I am grateful to God for everything! And I believe the point is to bring a little more colors, joy to all the little ones, and adults that can be a source of inspiration, thank you very much.

Ismael Castro
2023

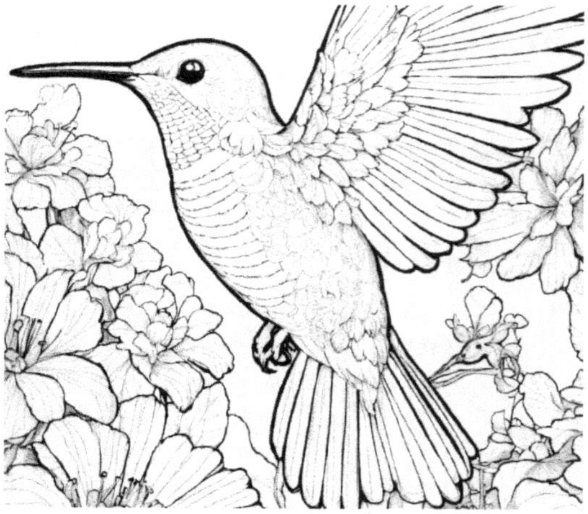
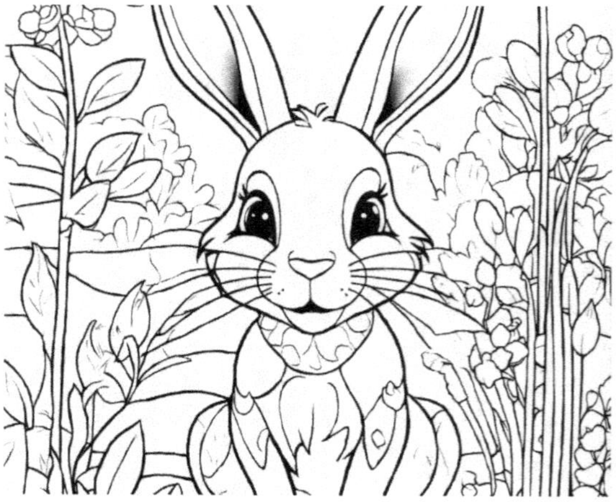

This Book Belongs to:

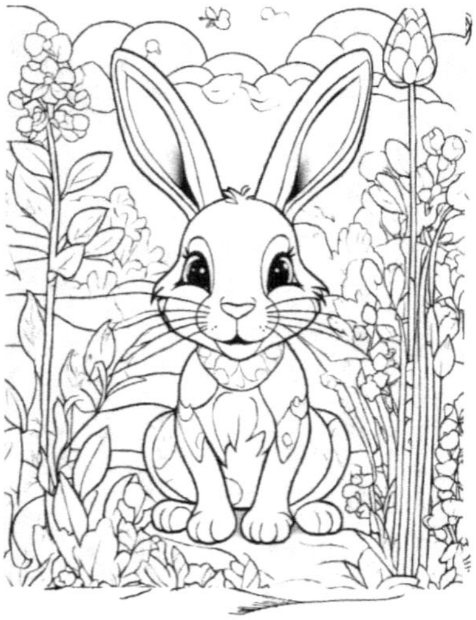
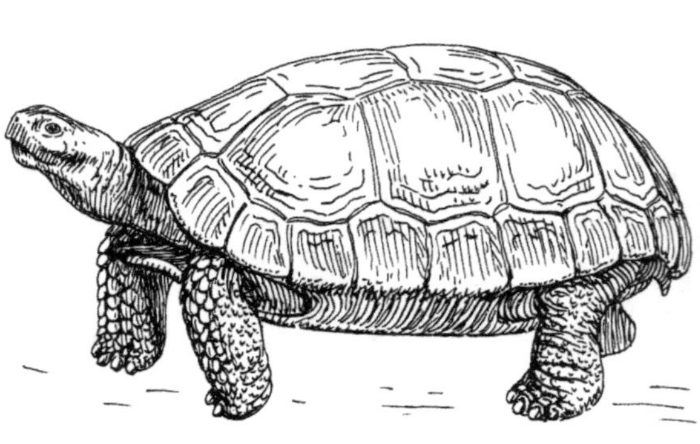

I.C.S.©
publications by Ismael Castro

Test Color Page

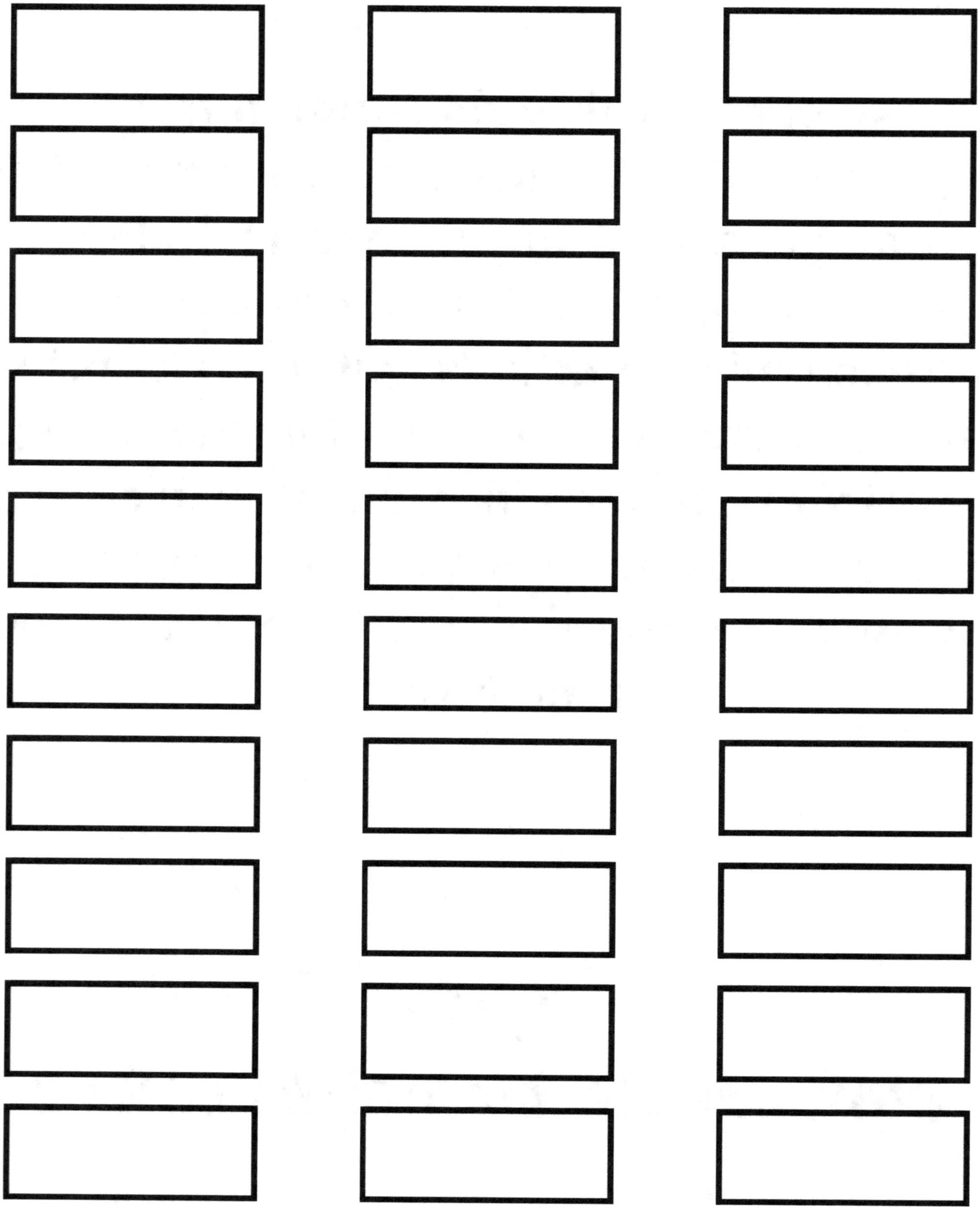

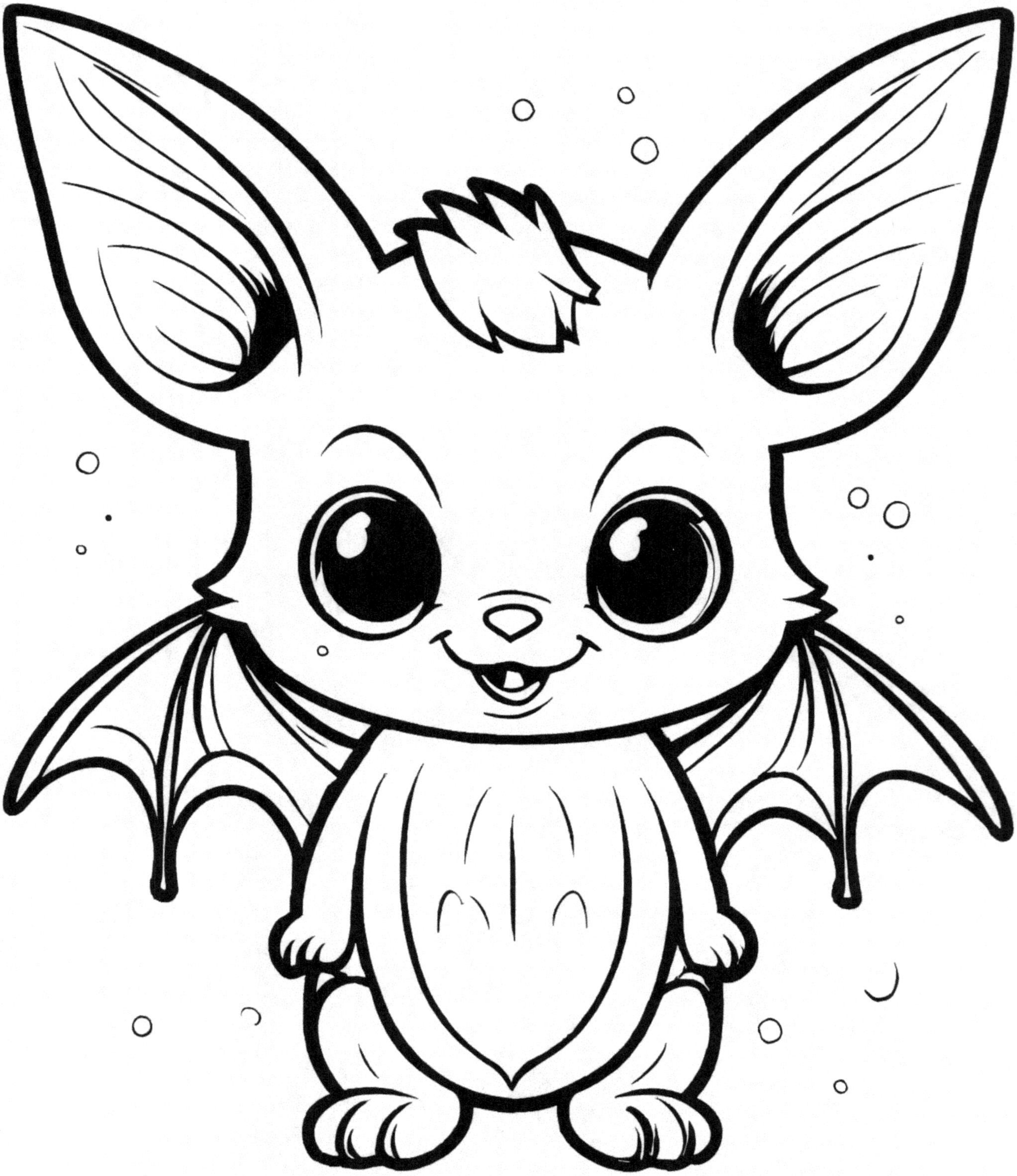

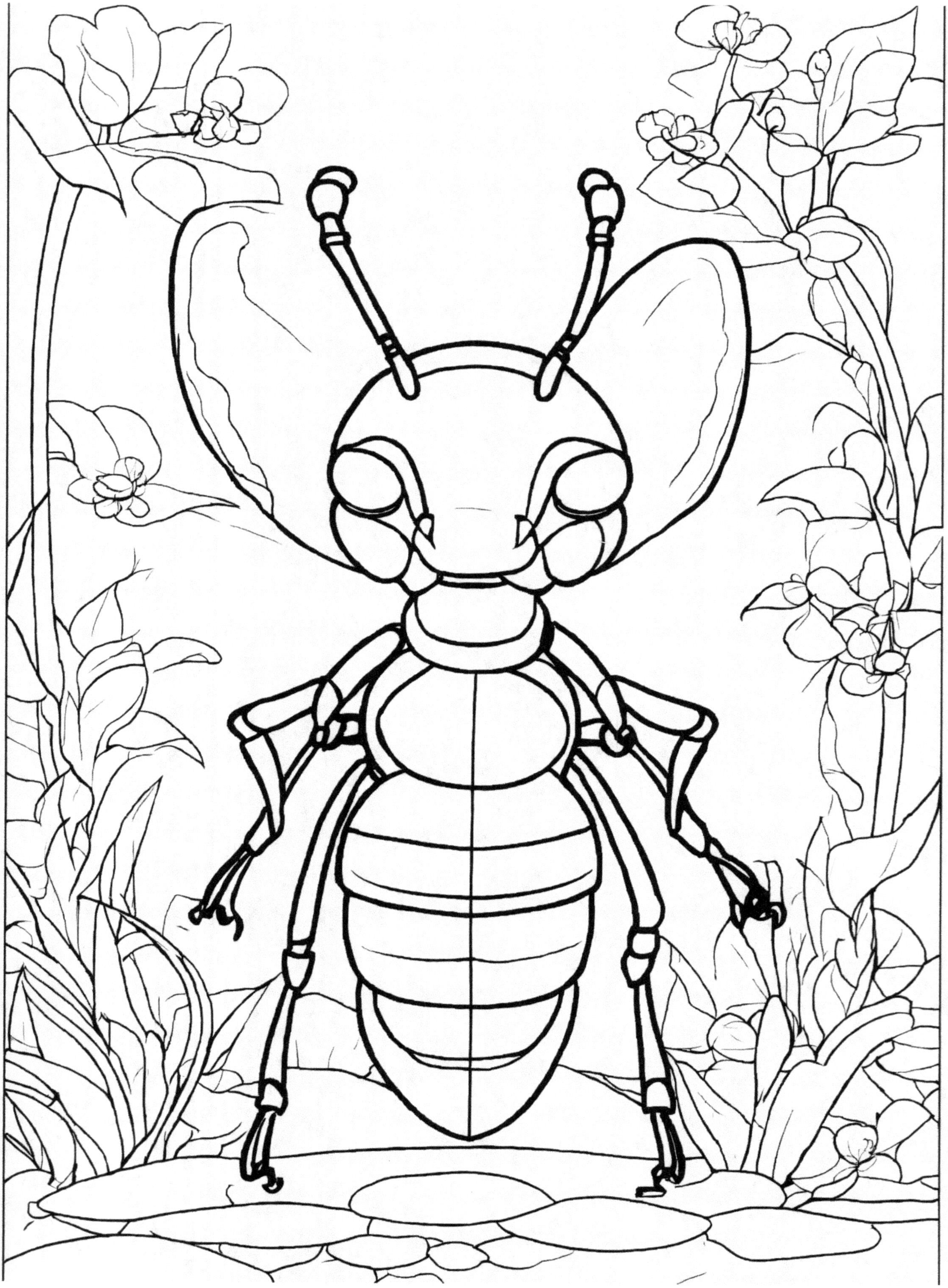

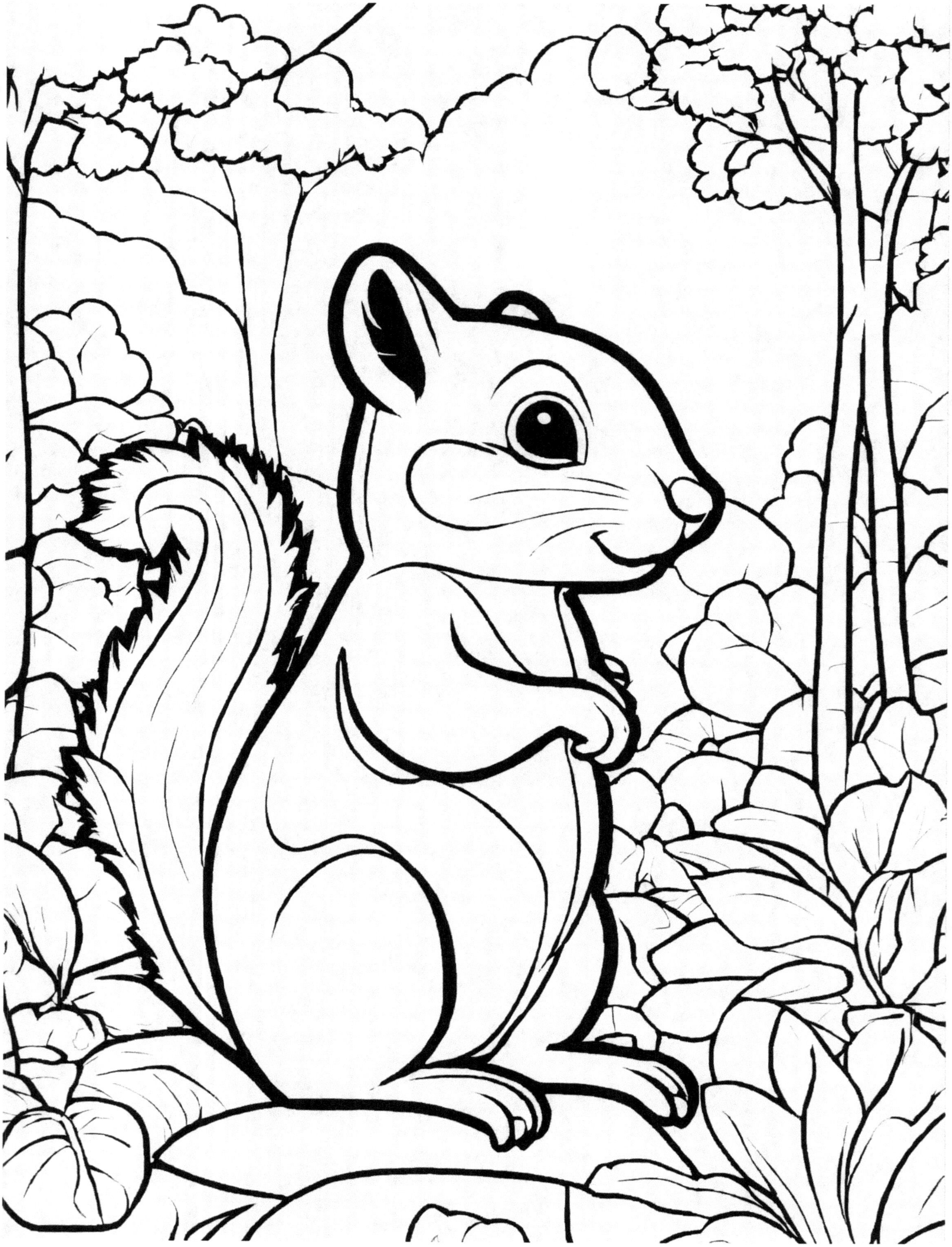

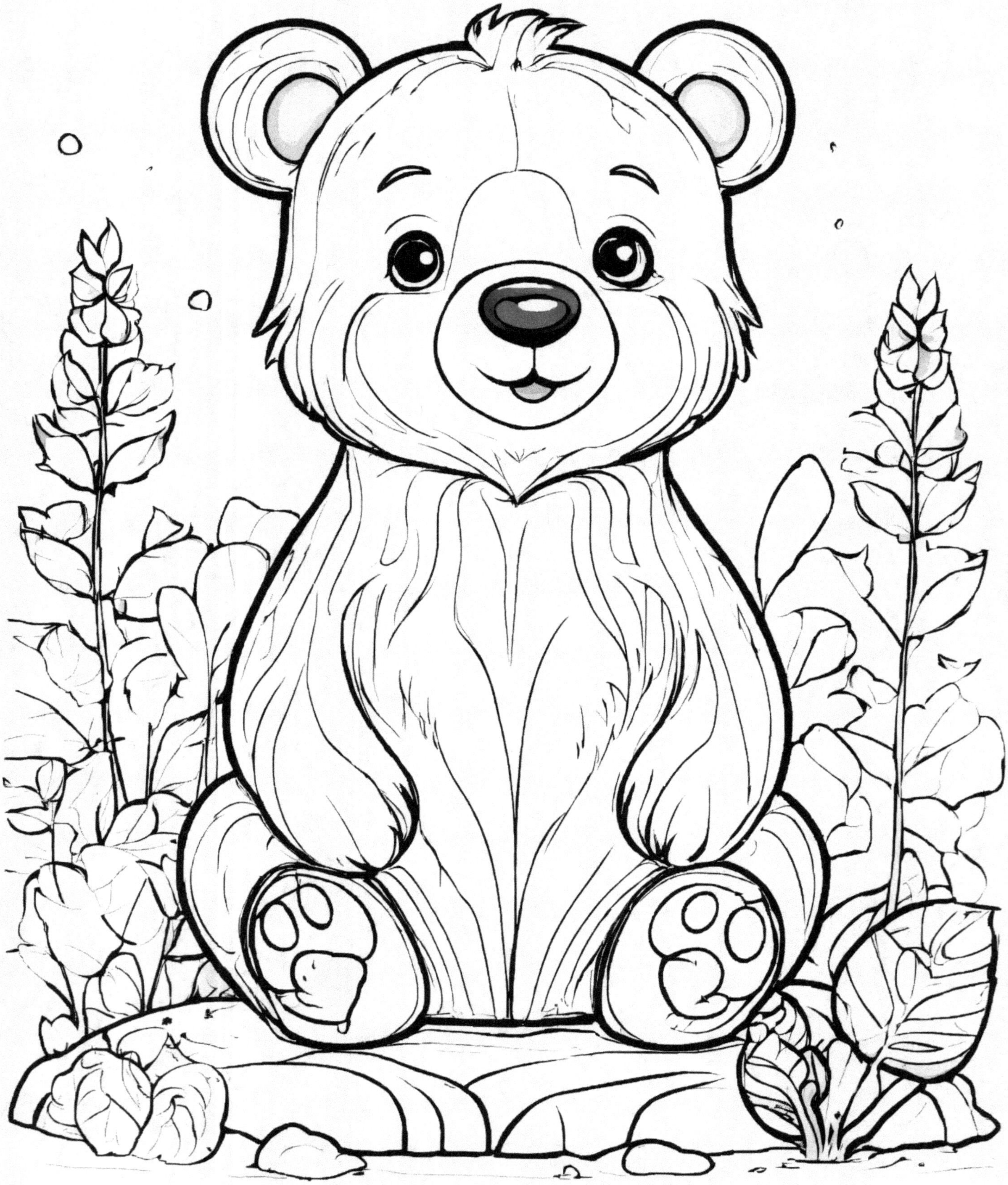

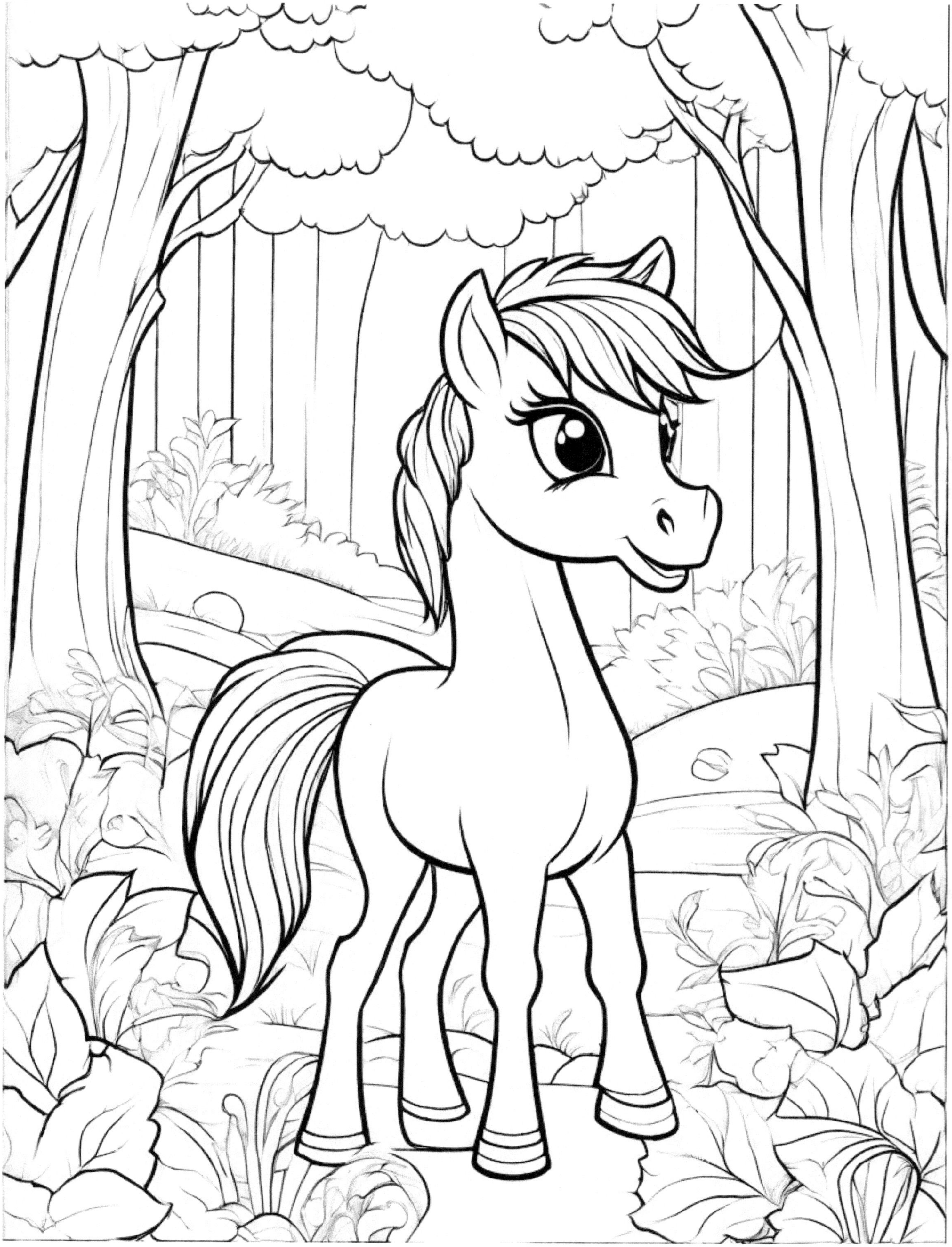

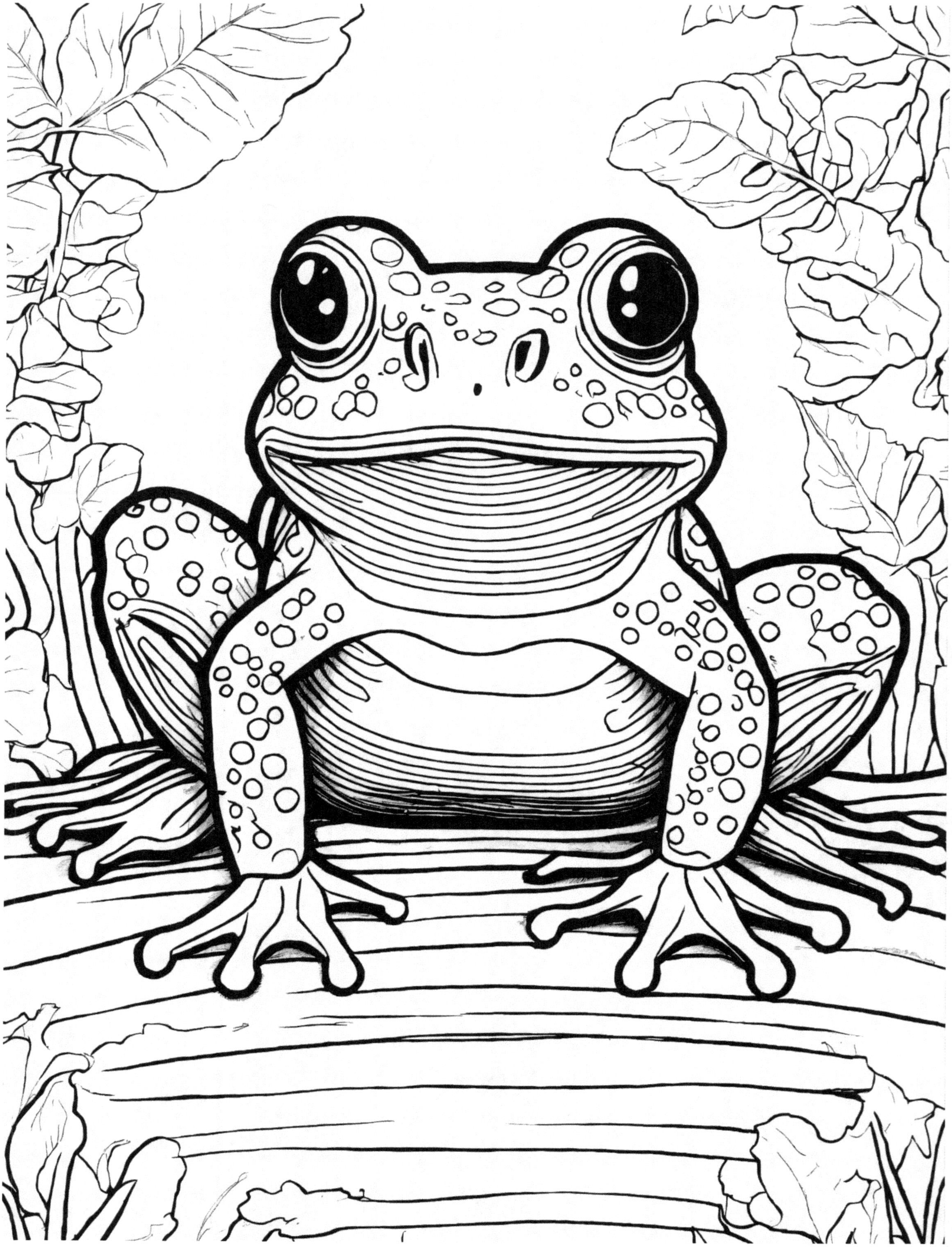

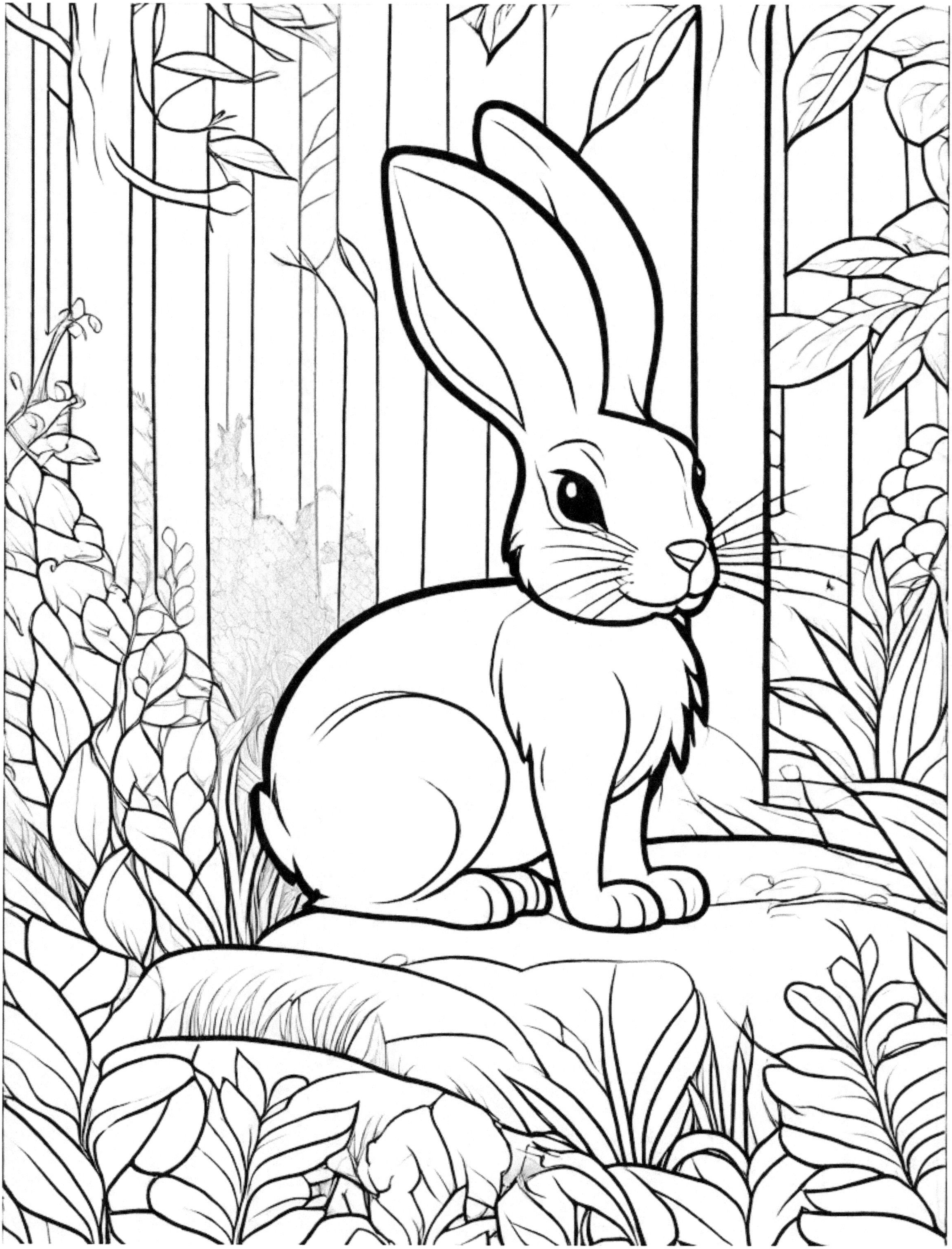

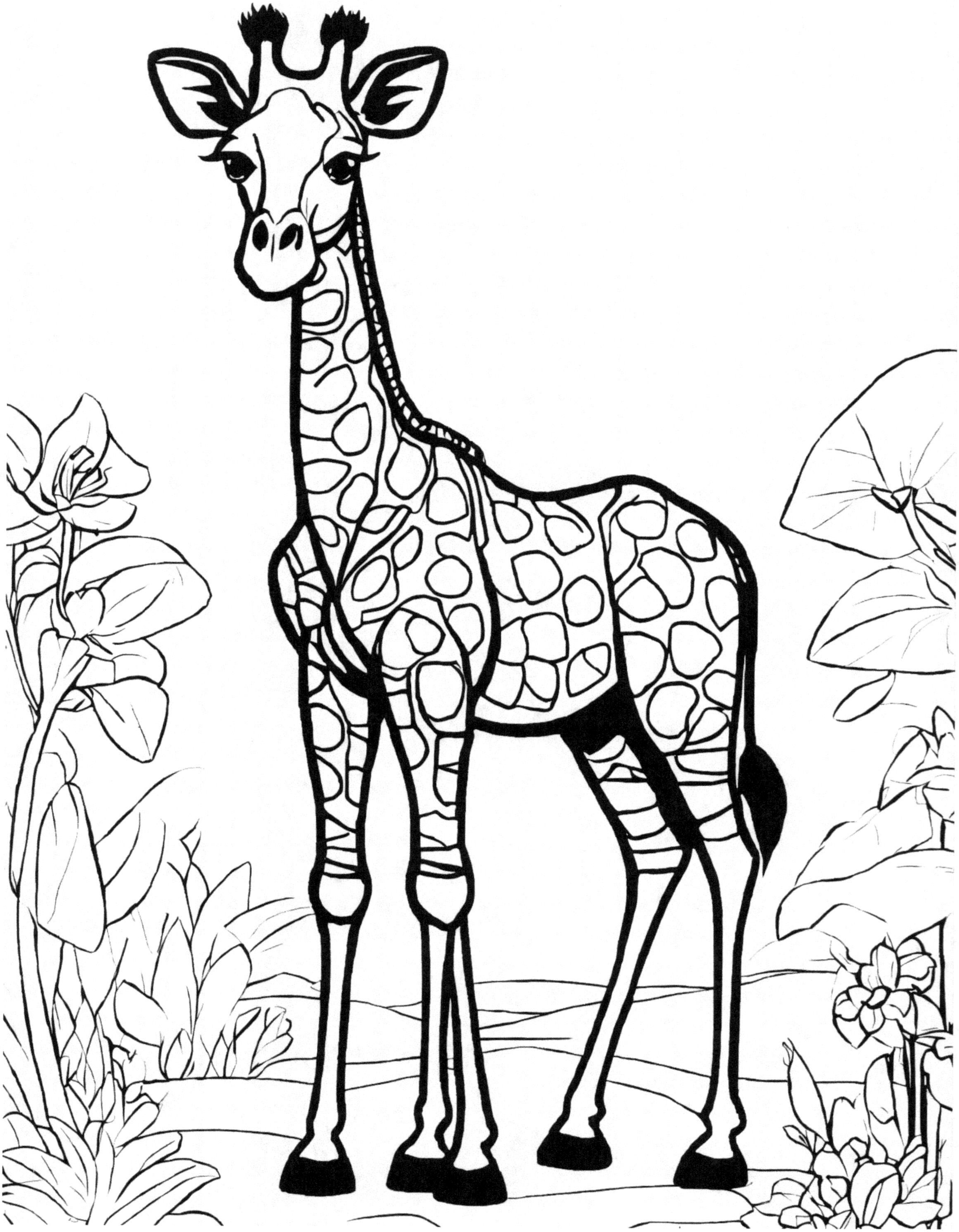

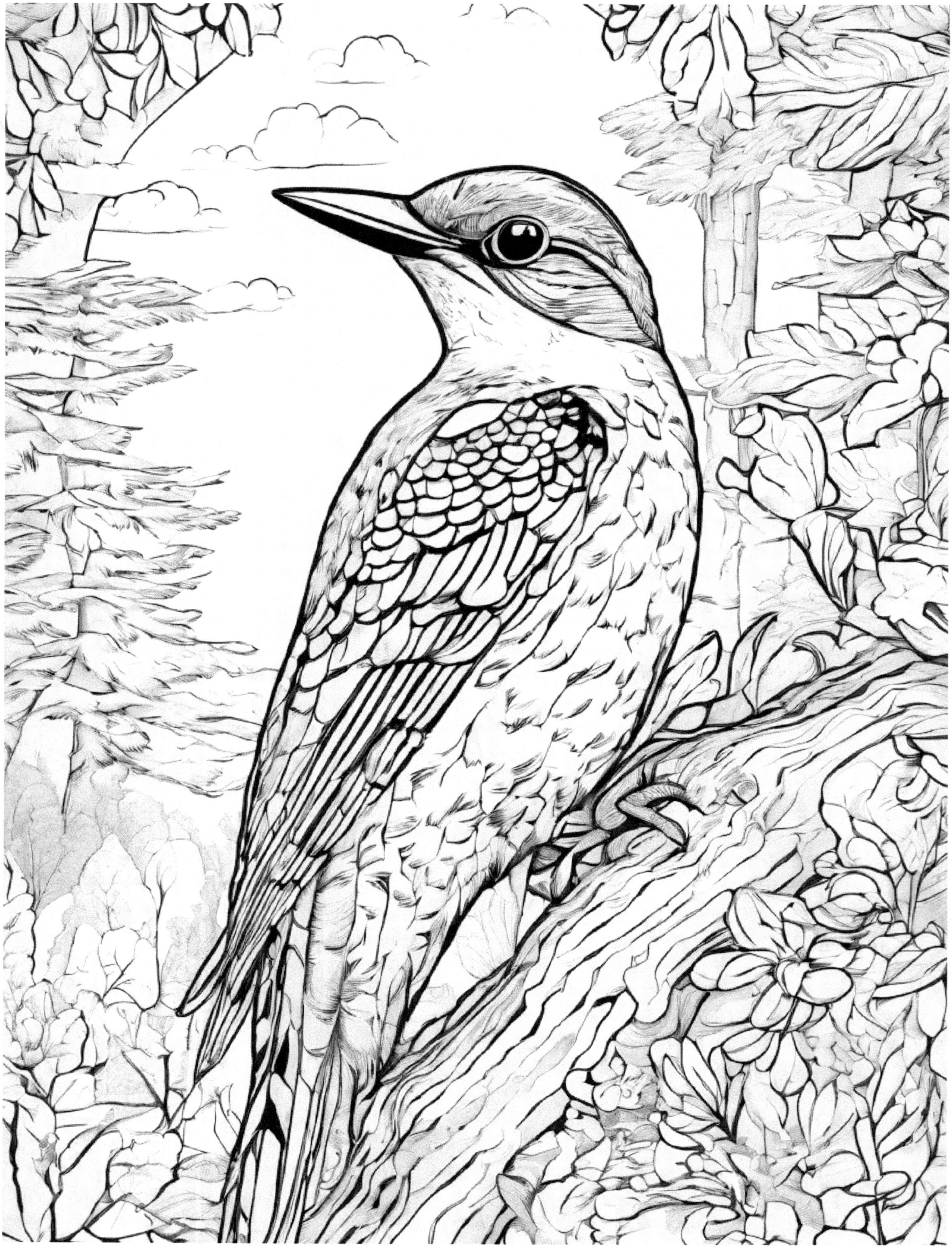

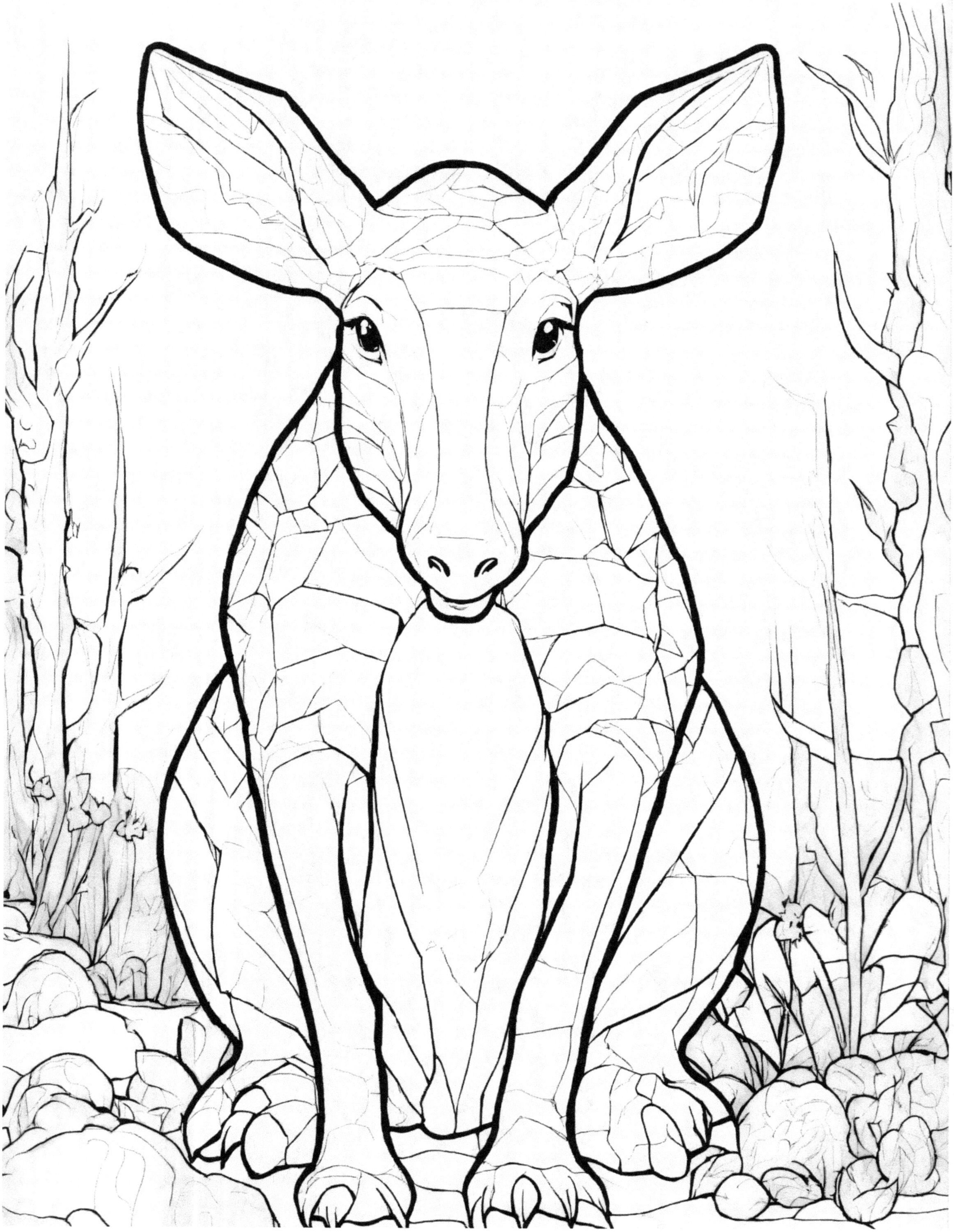

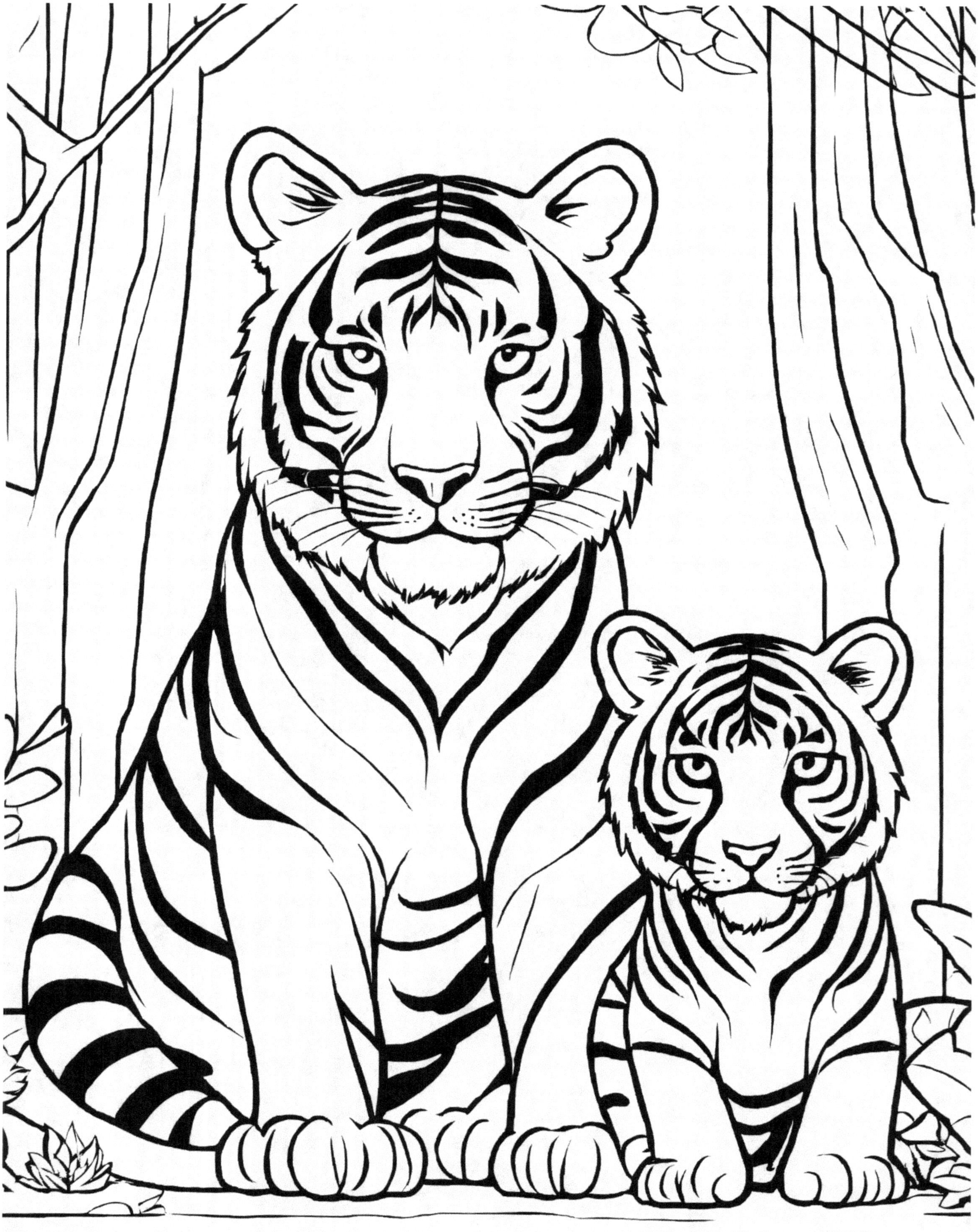

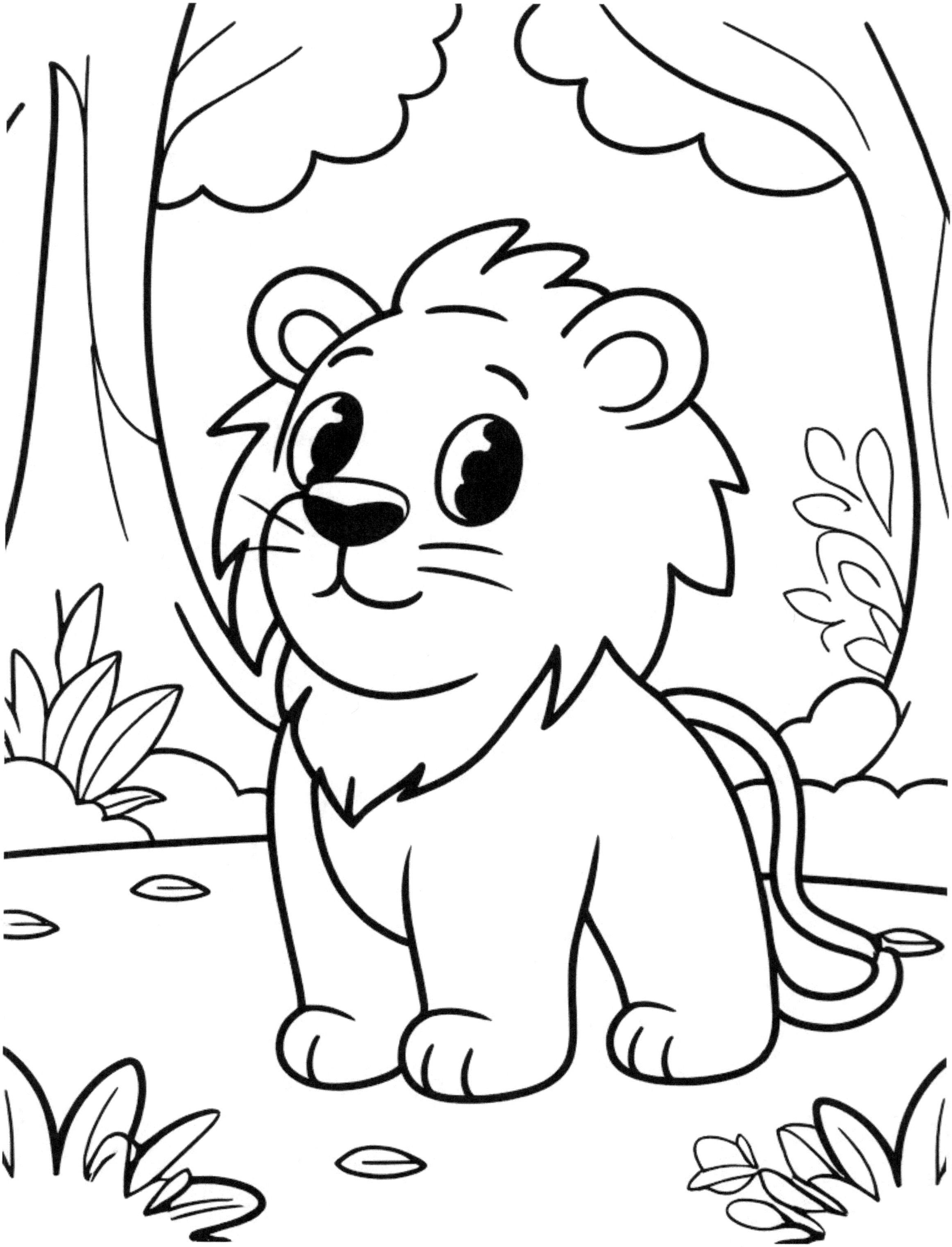

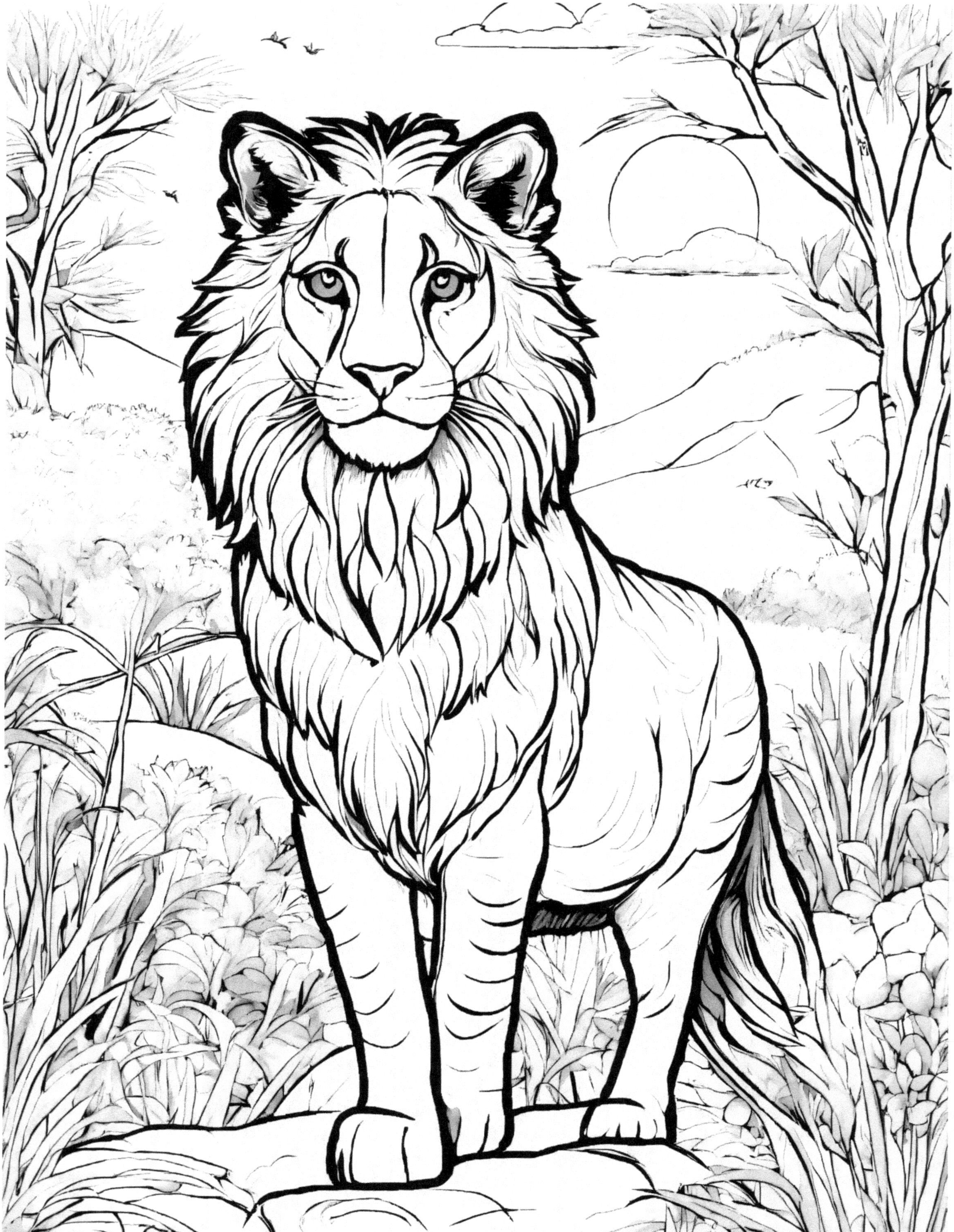

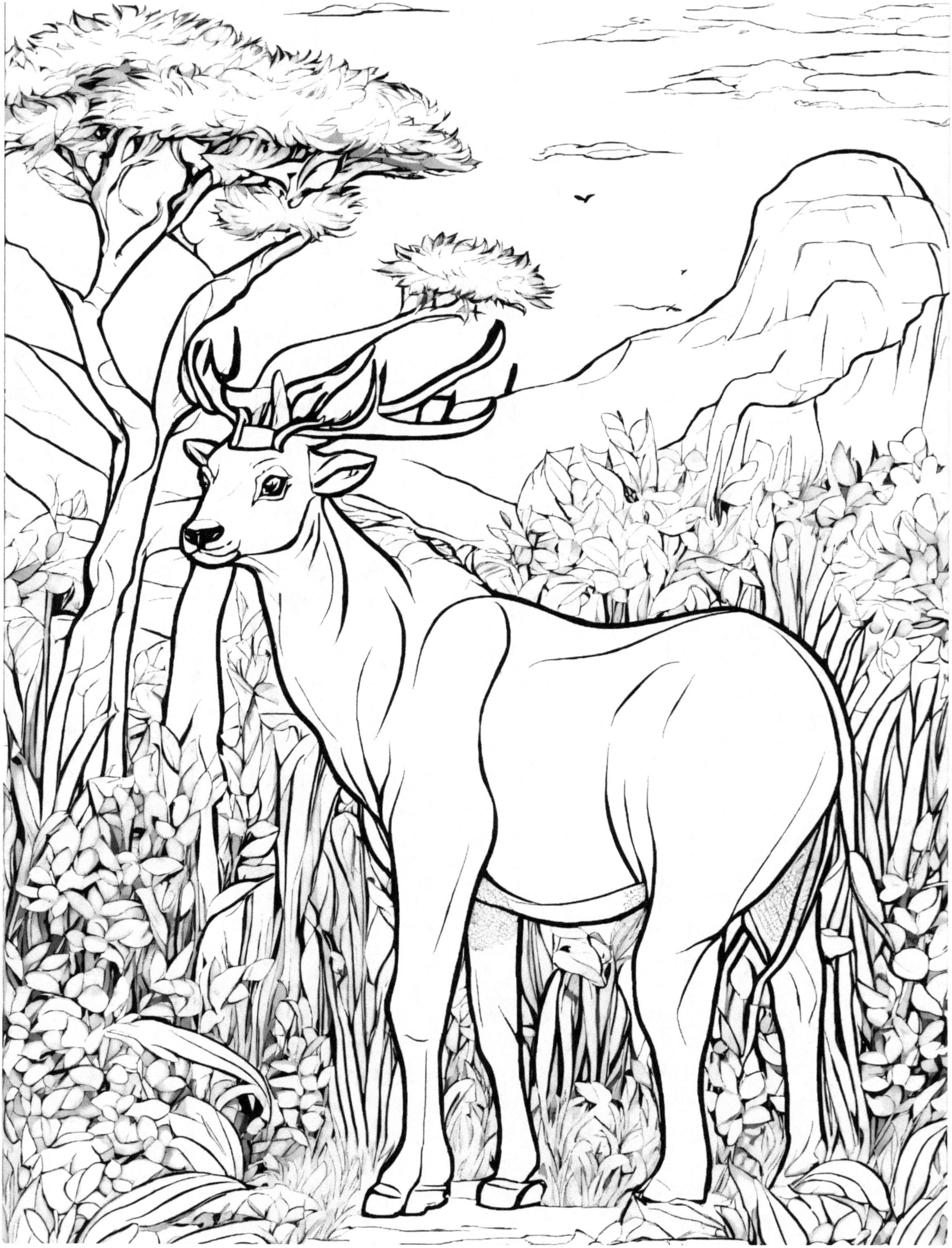

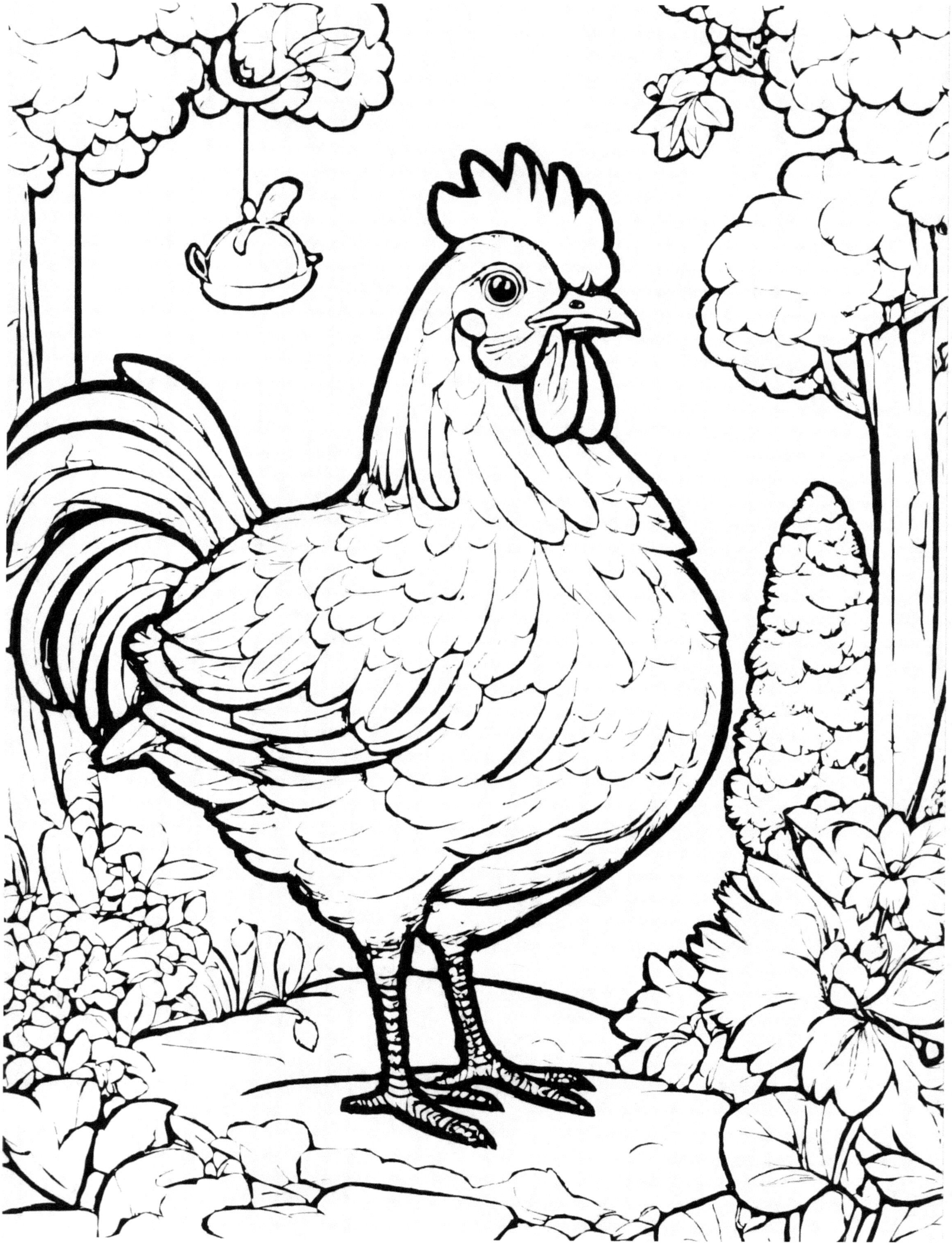

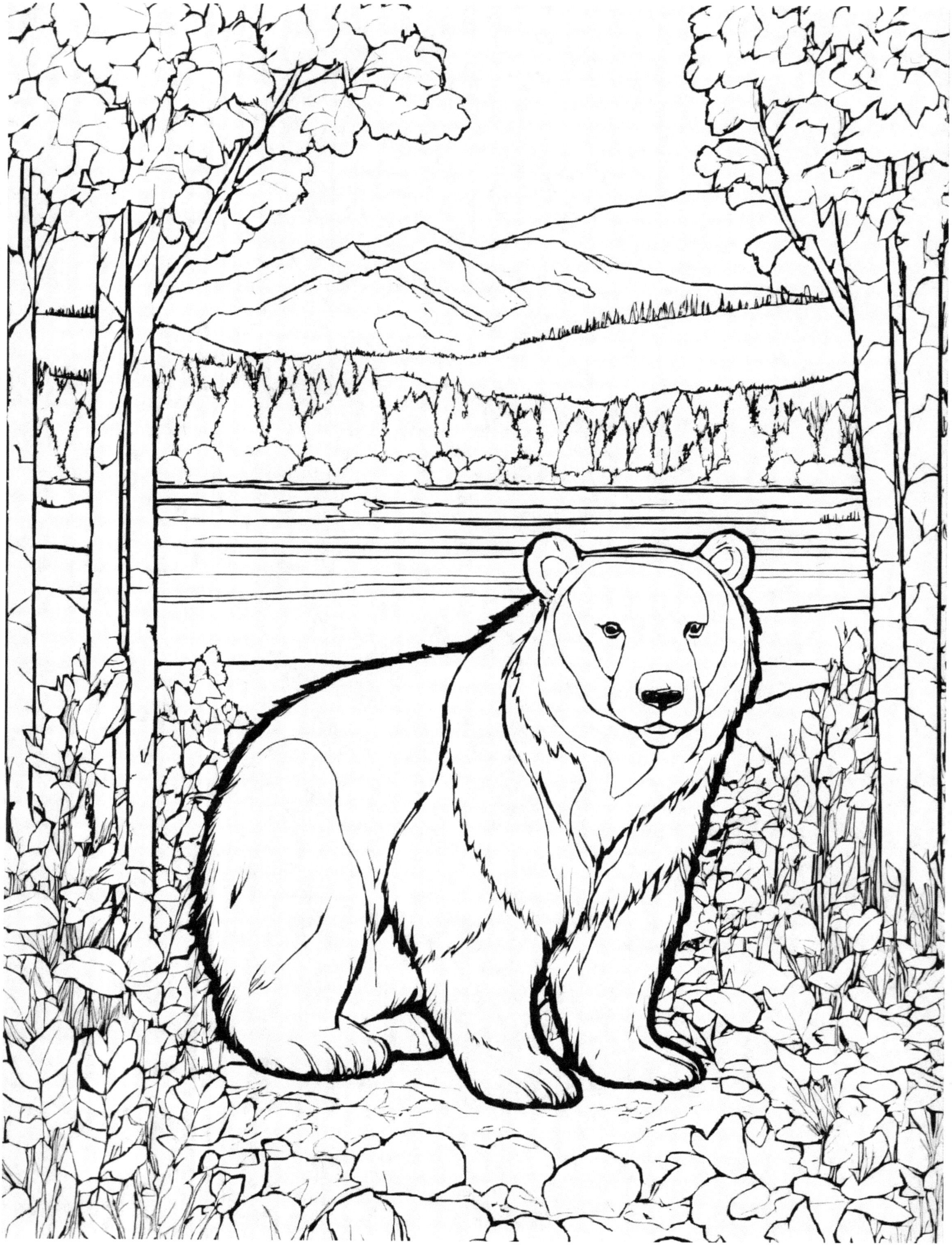

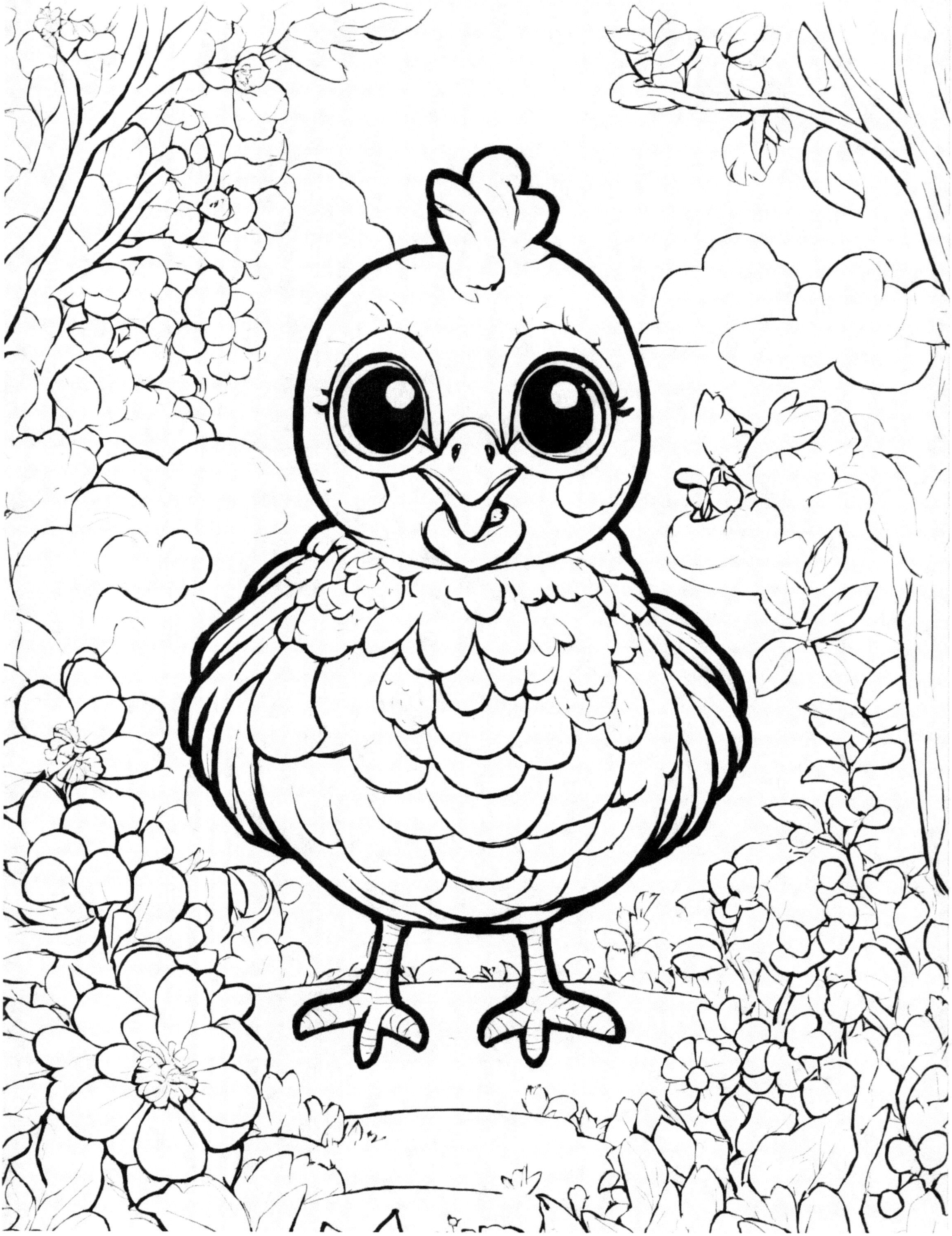

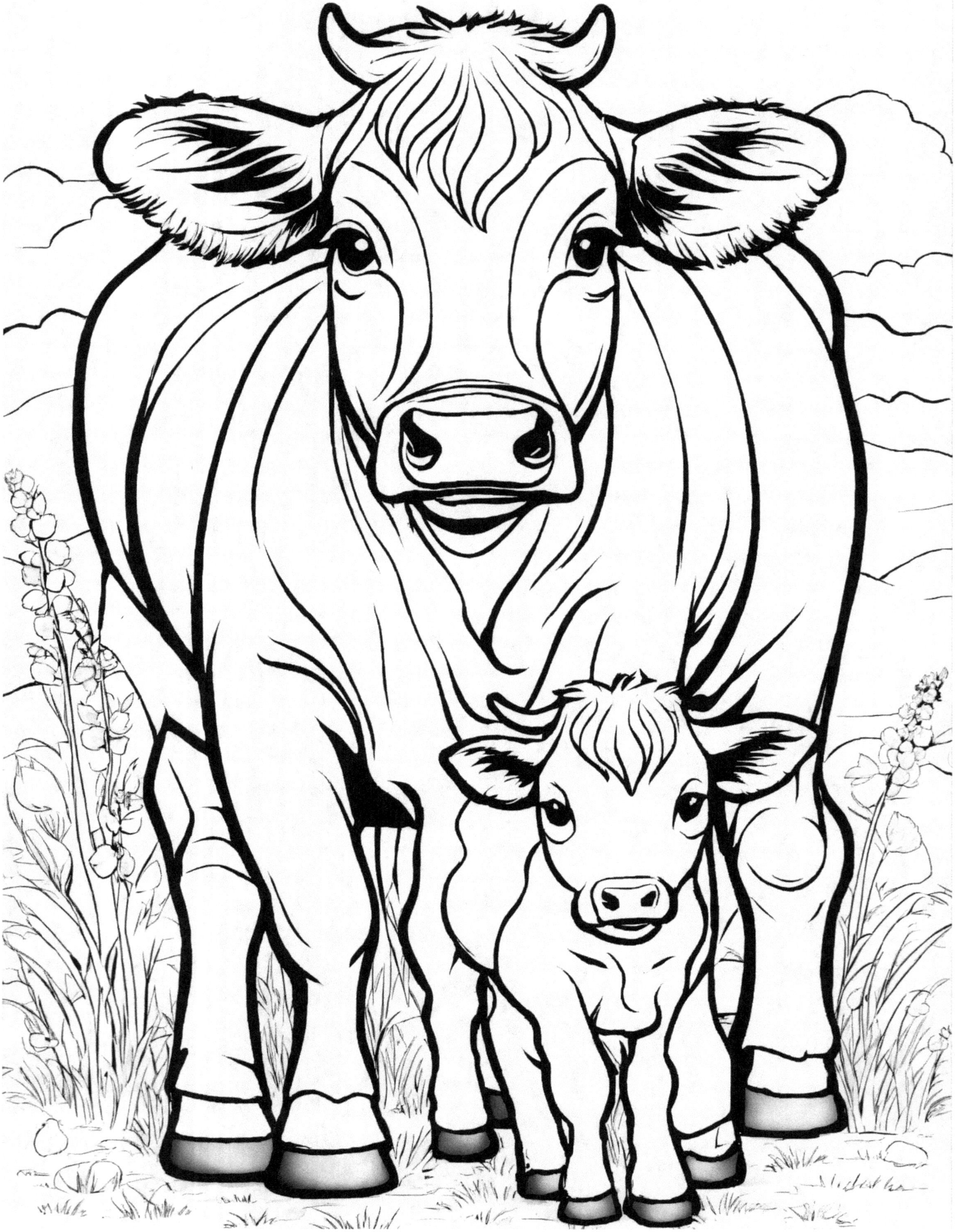

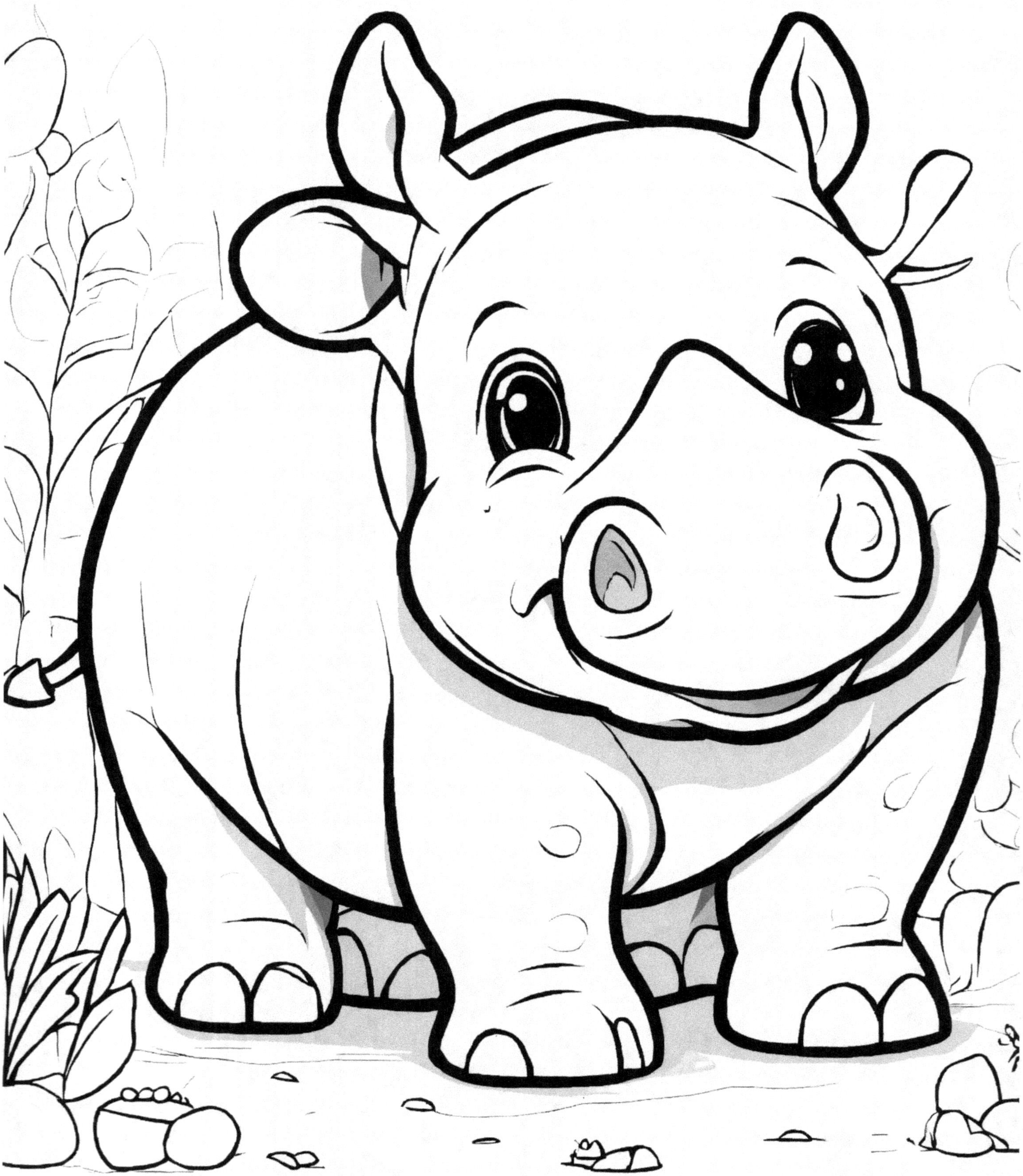

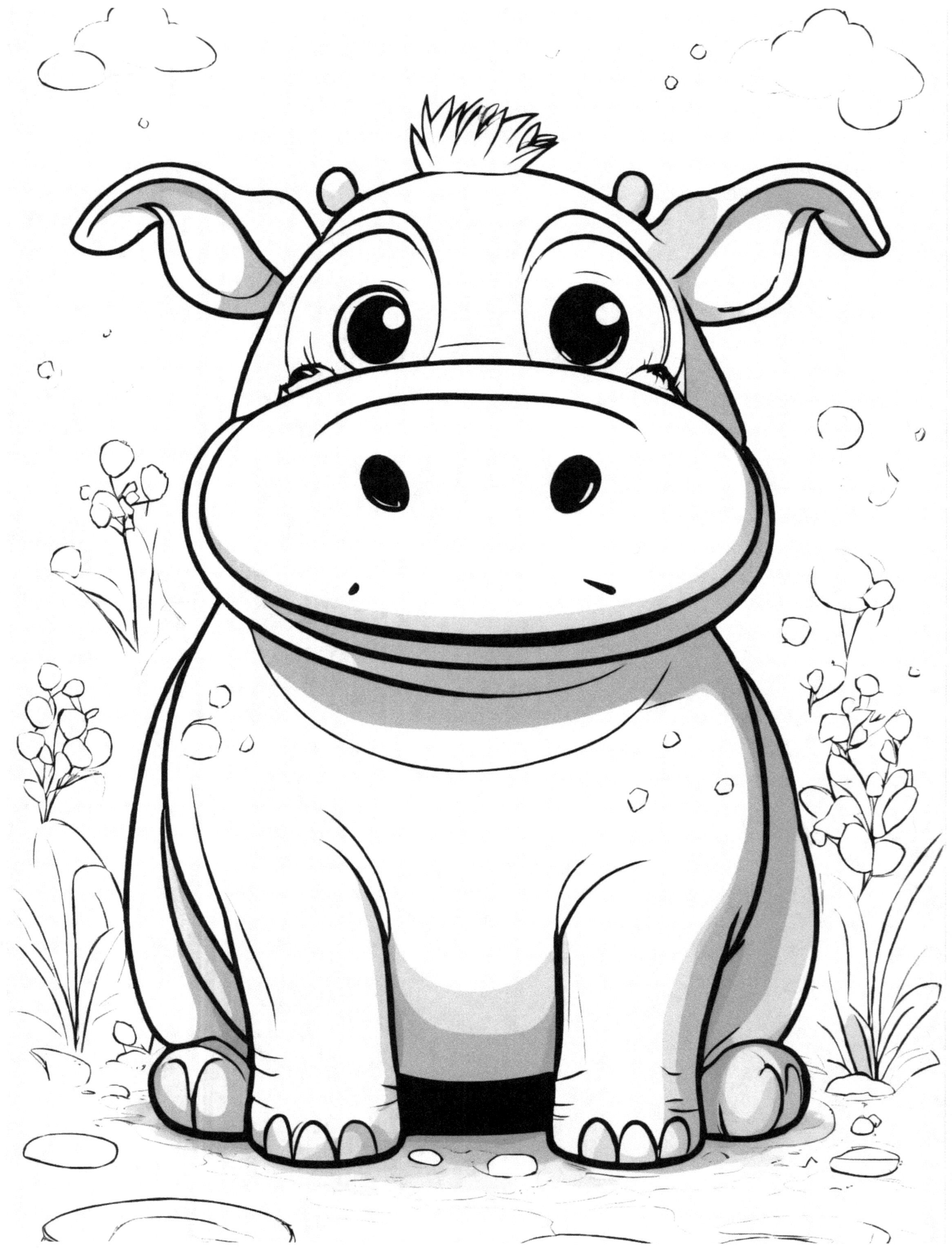

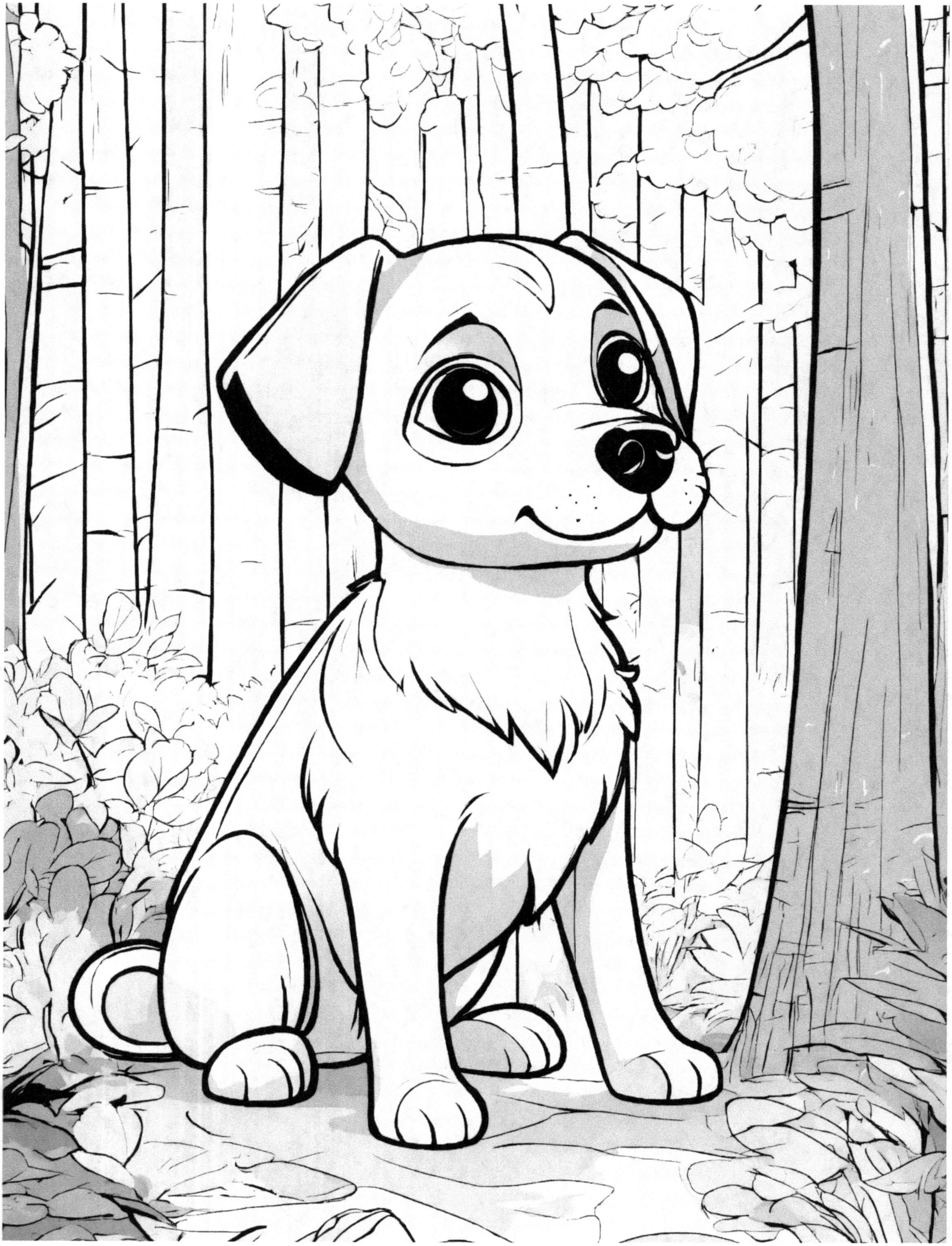

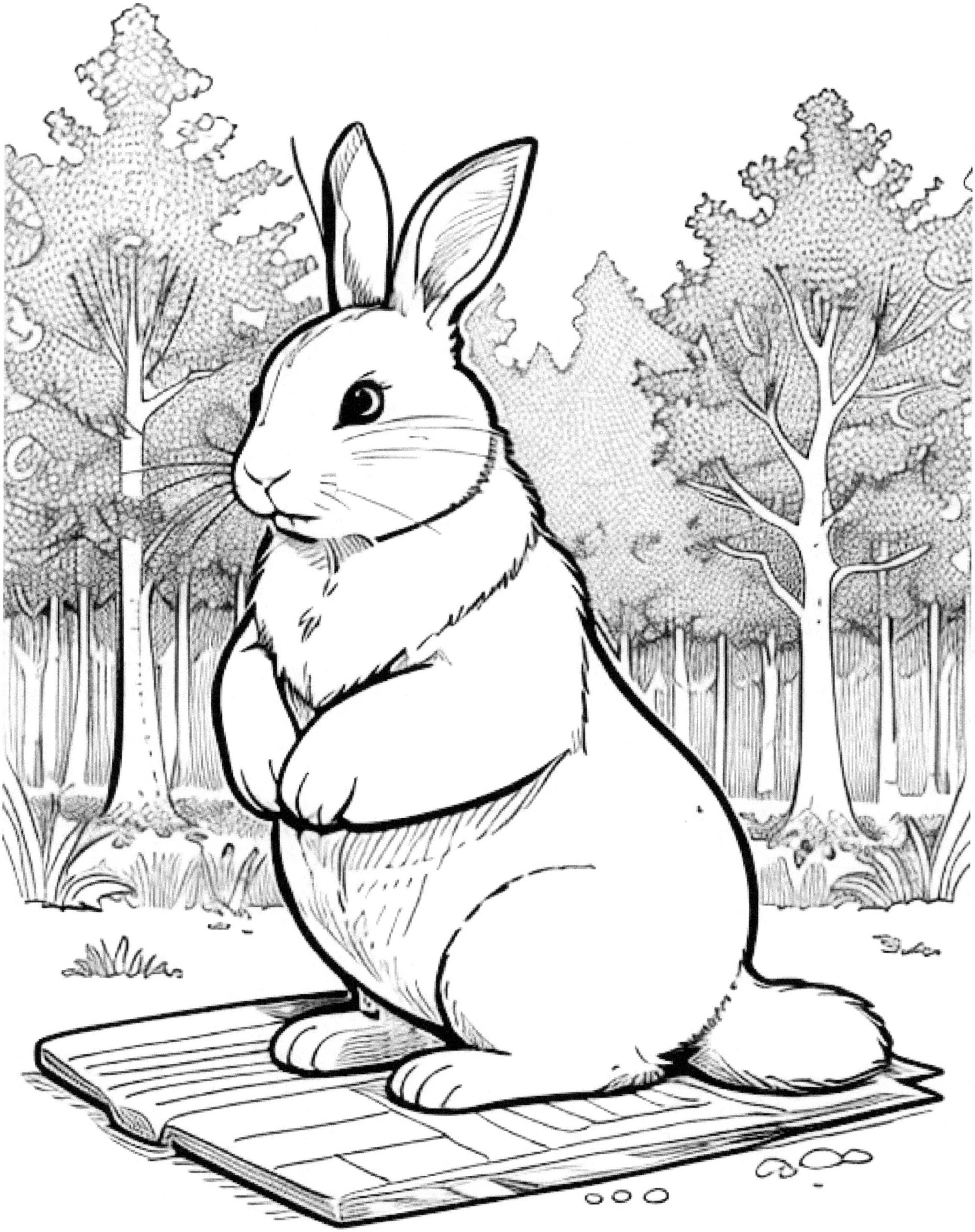

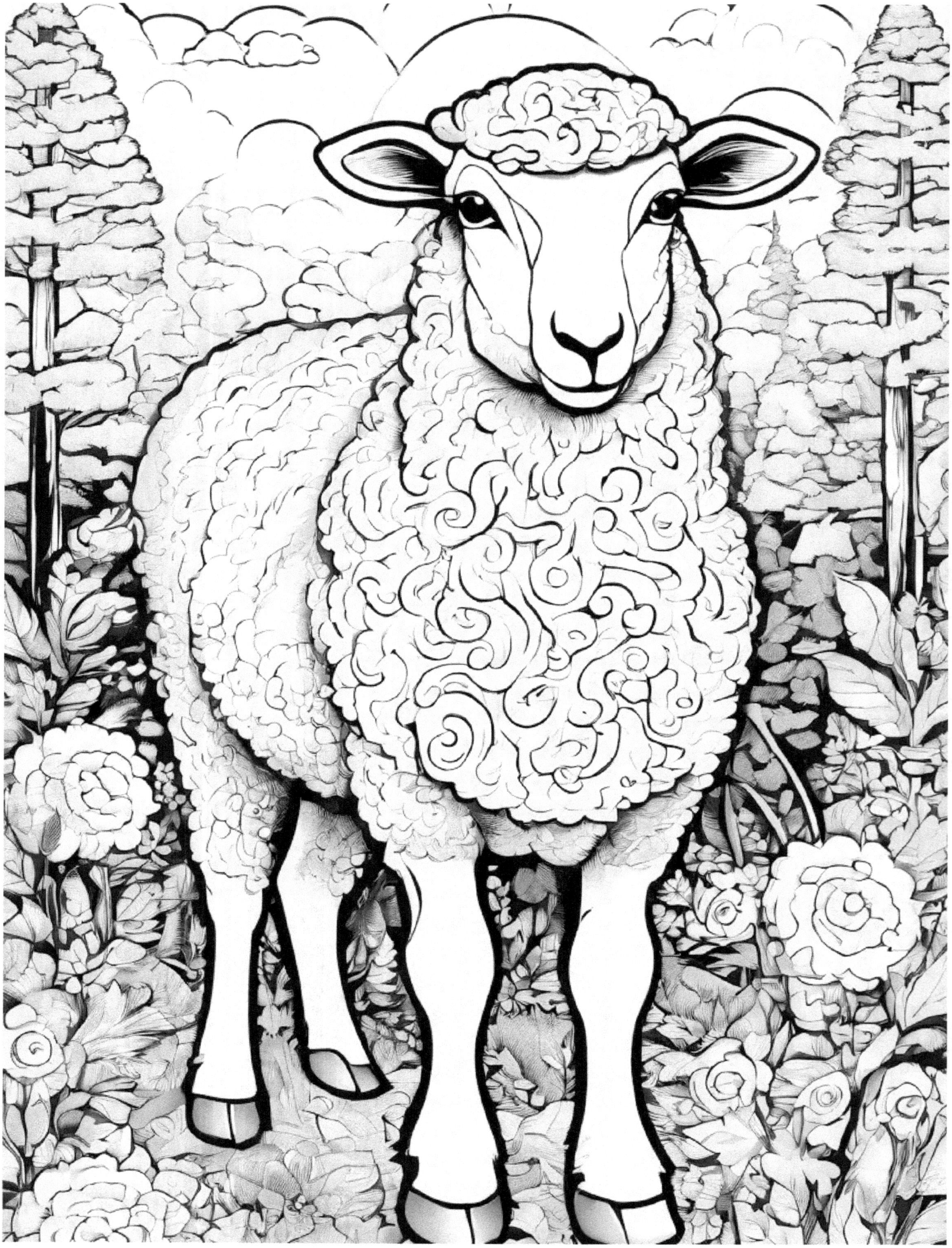

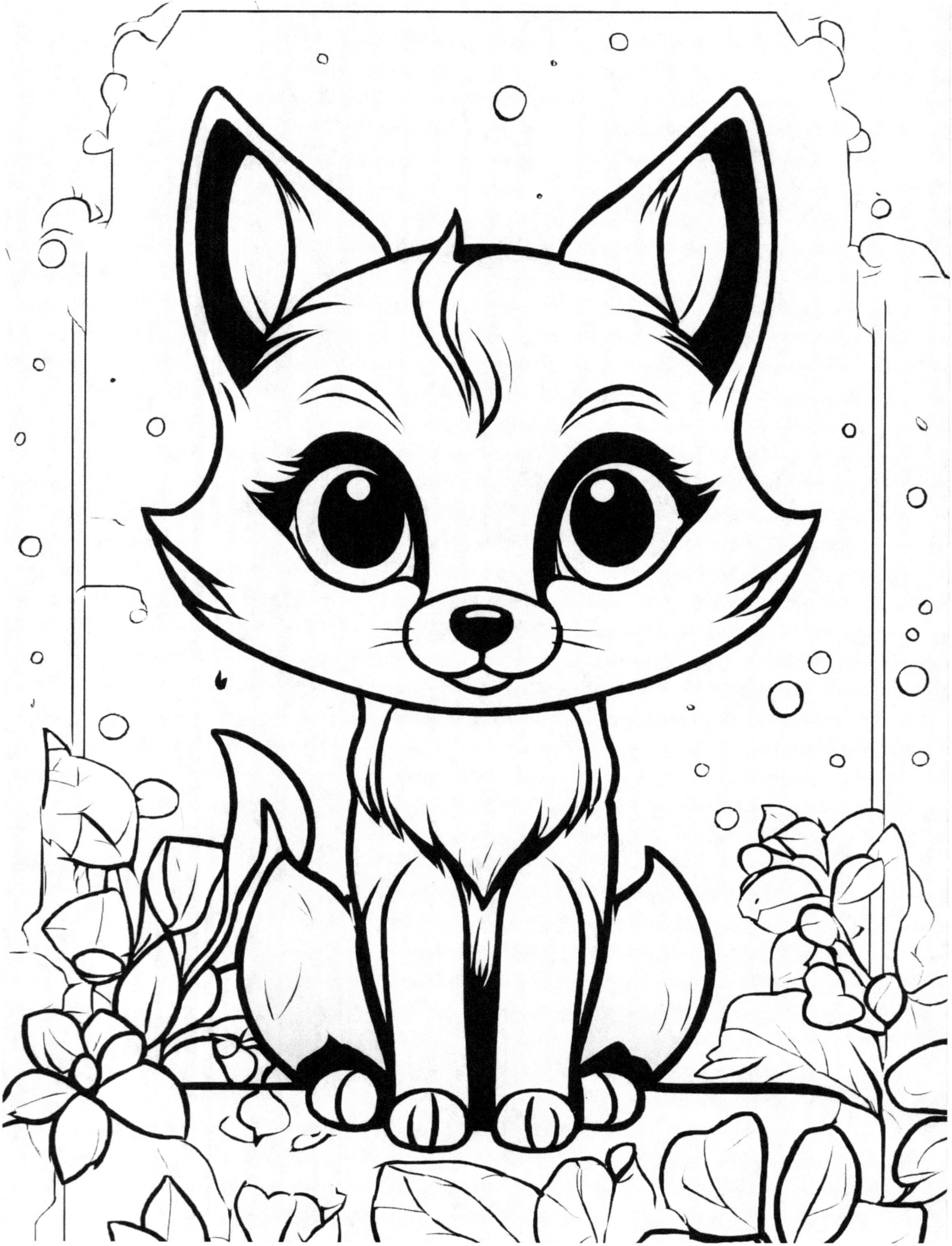

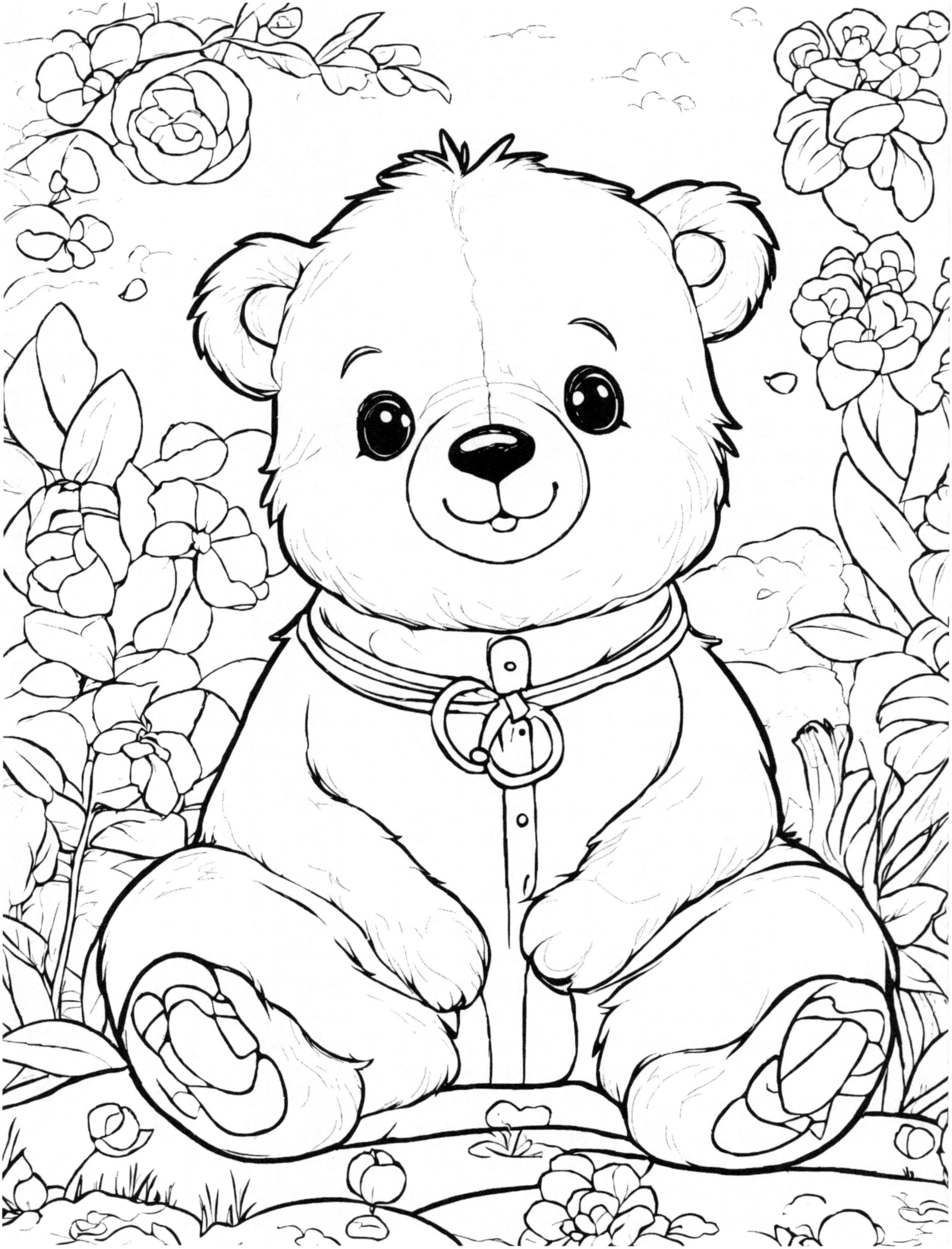

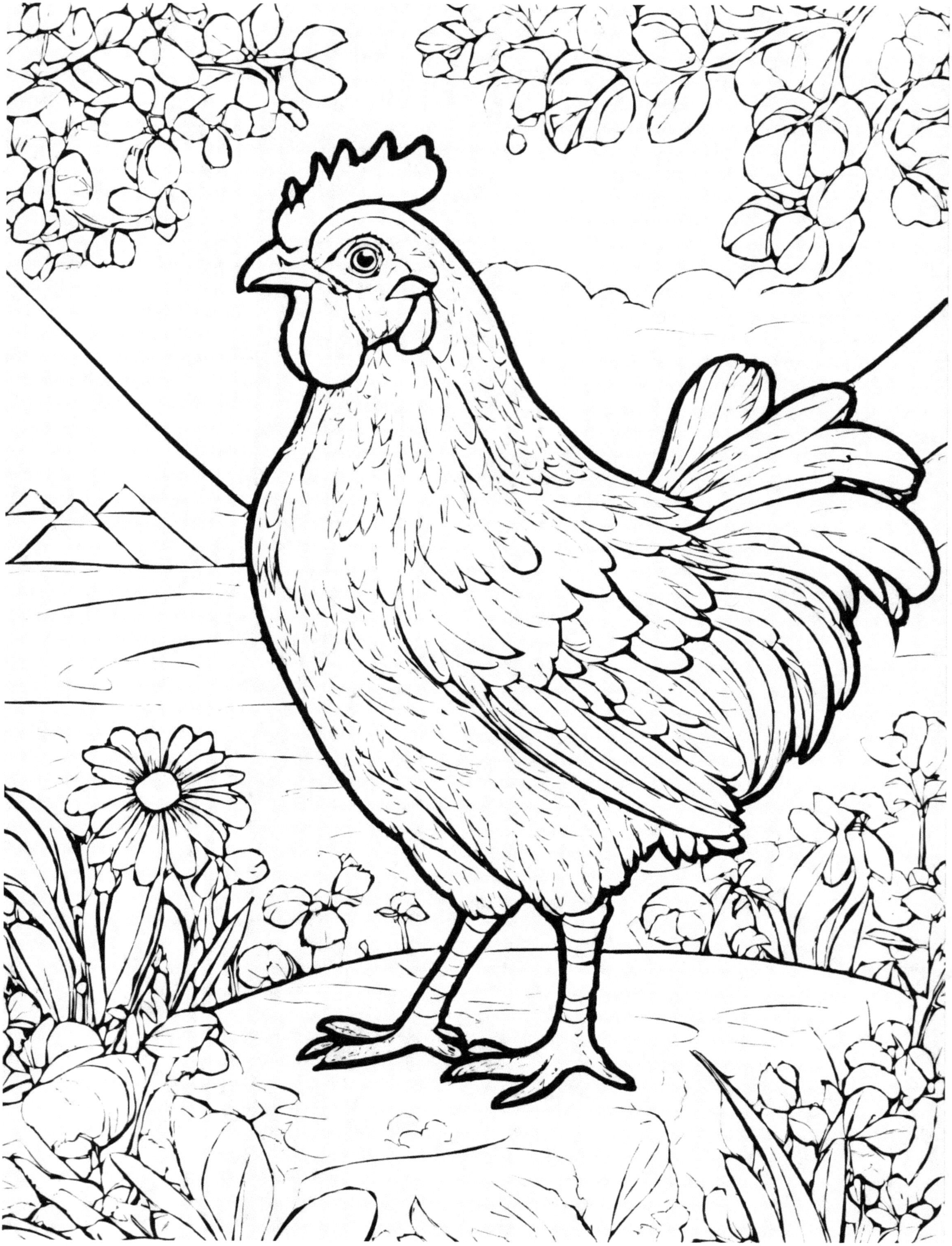

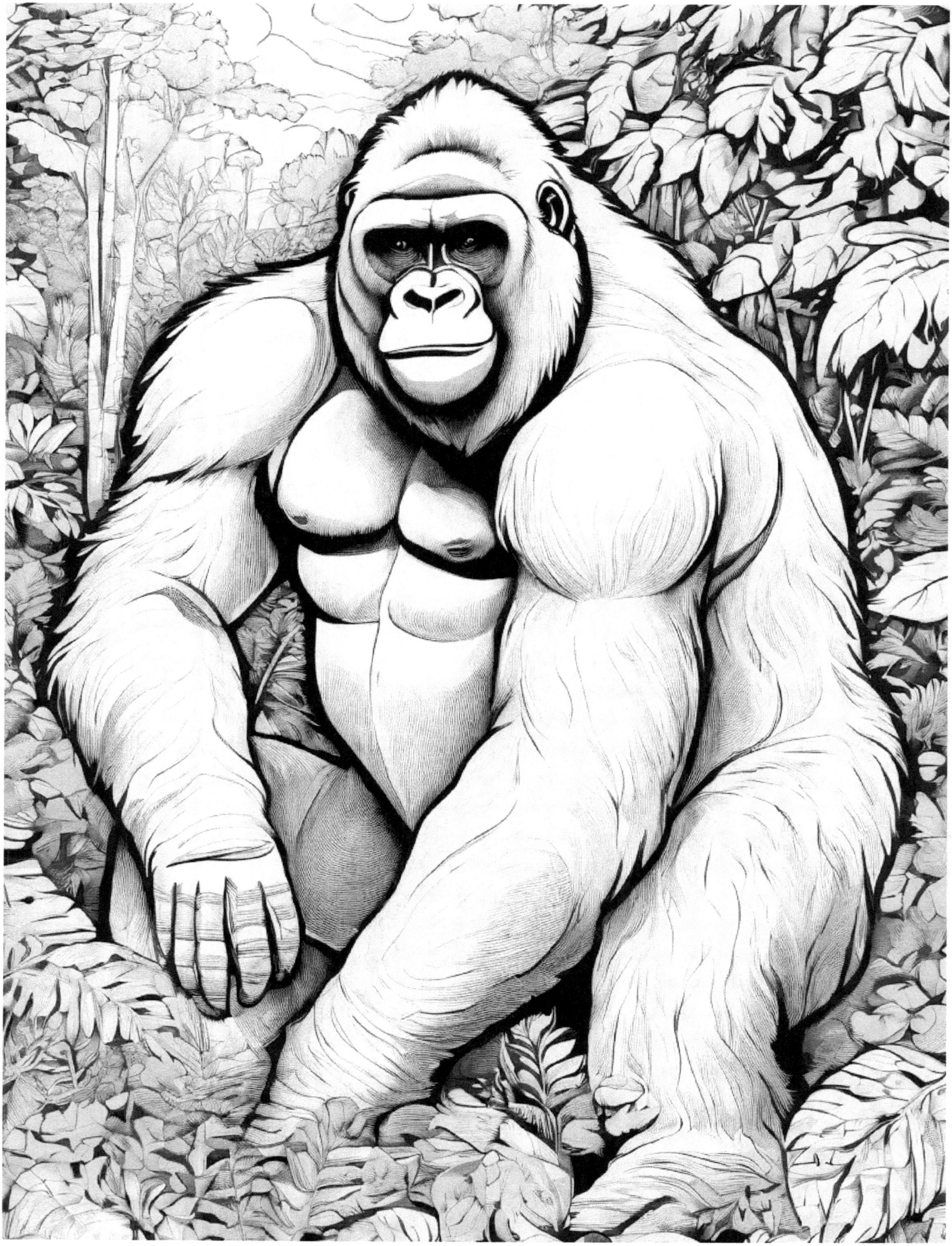

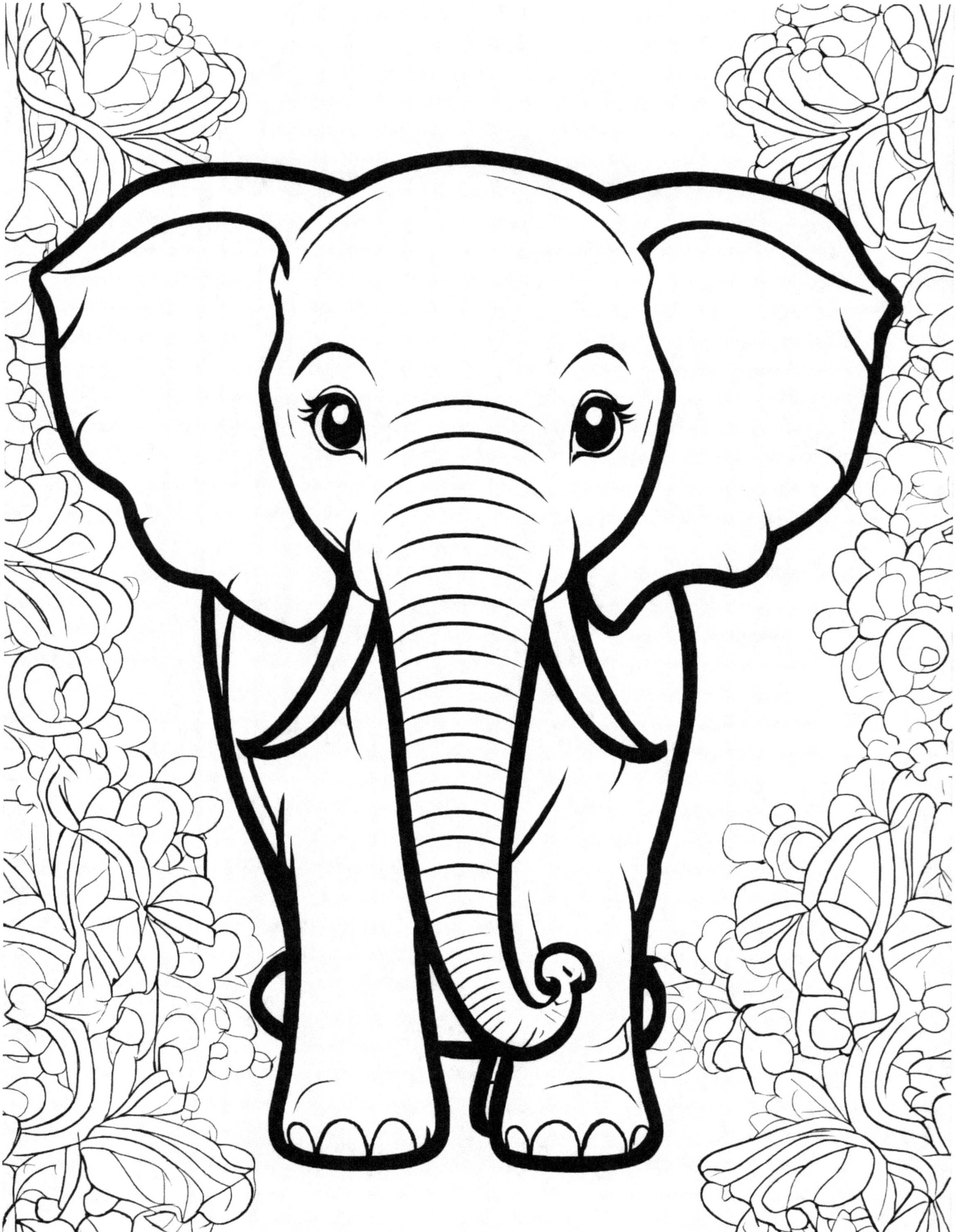

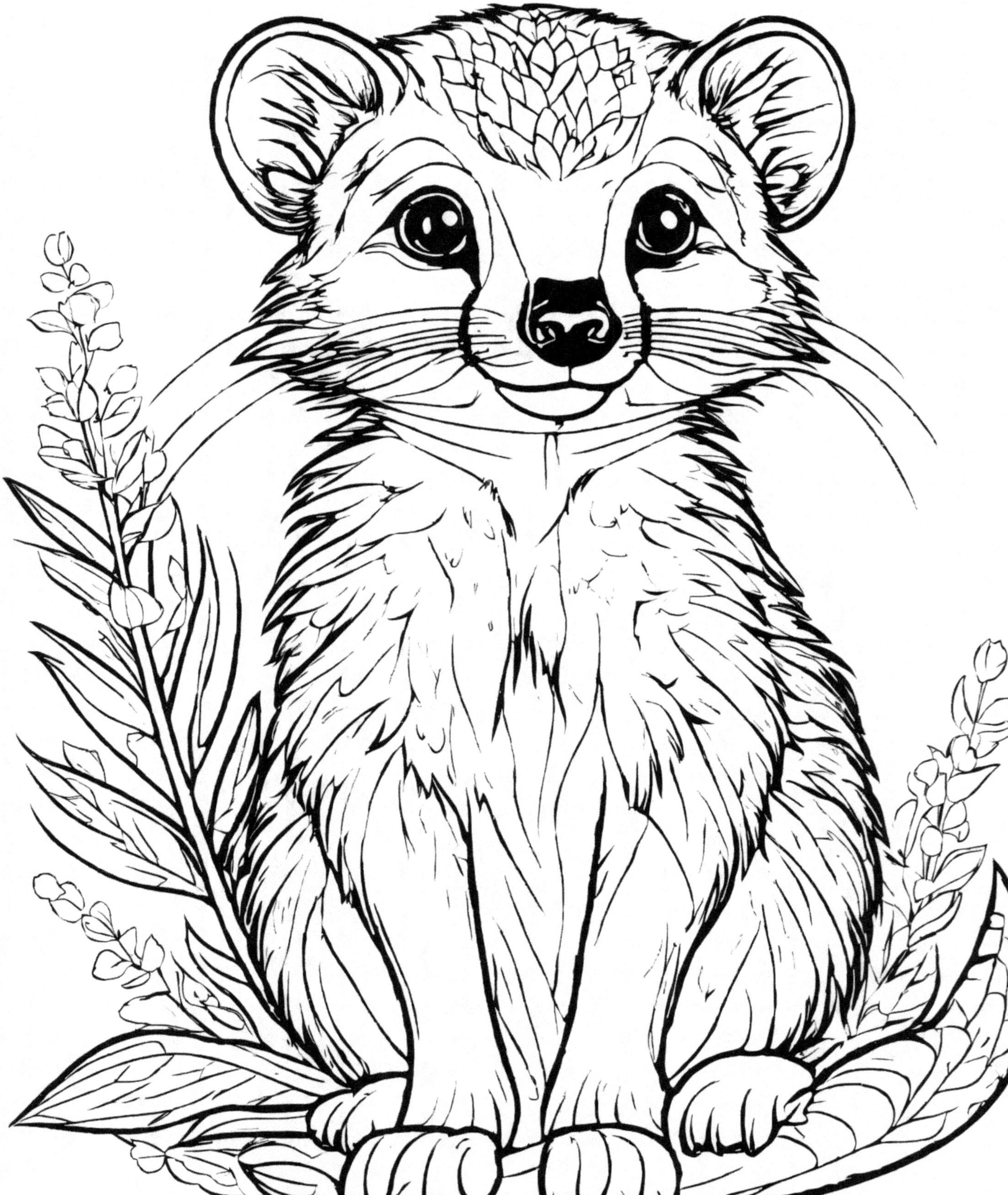

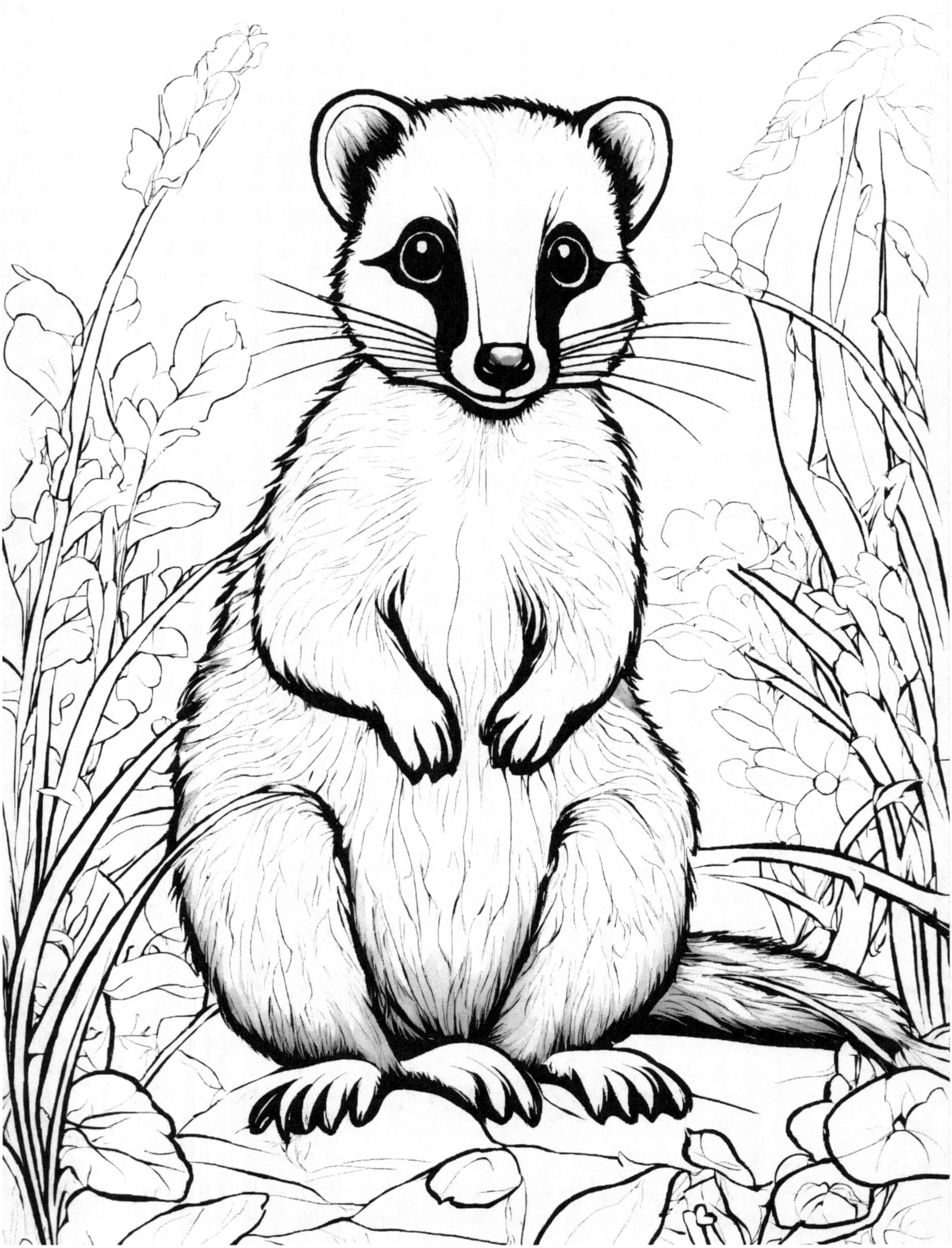

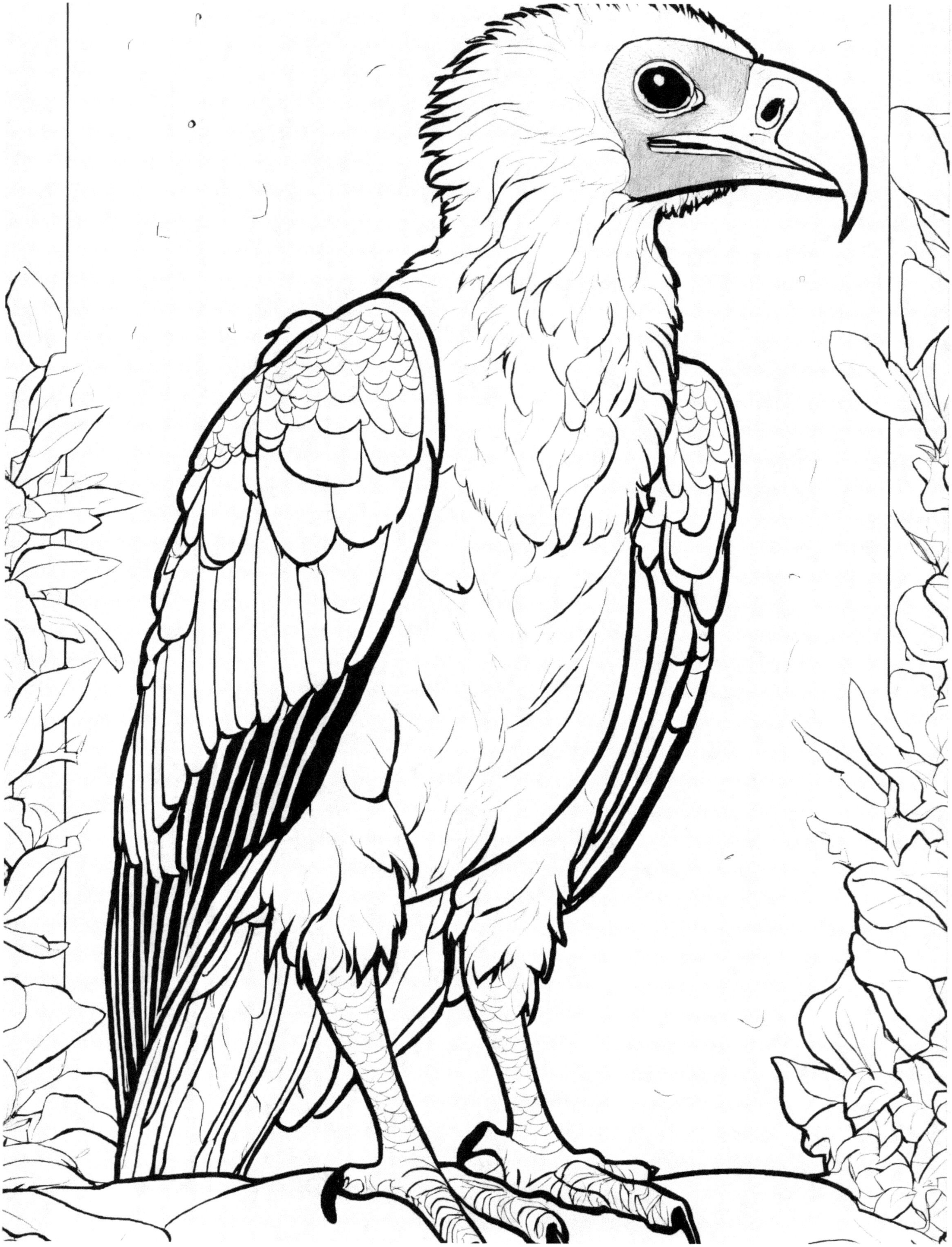

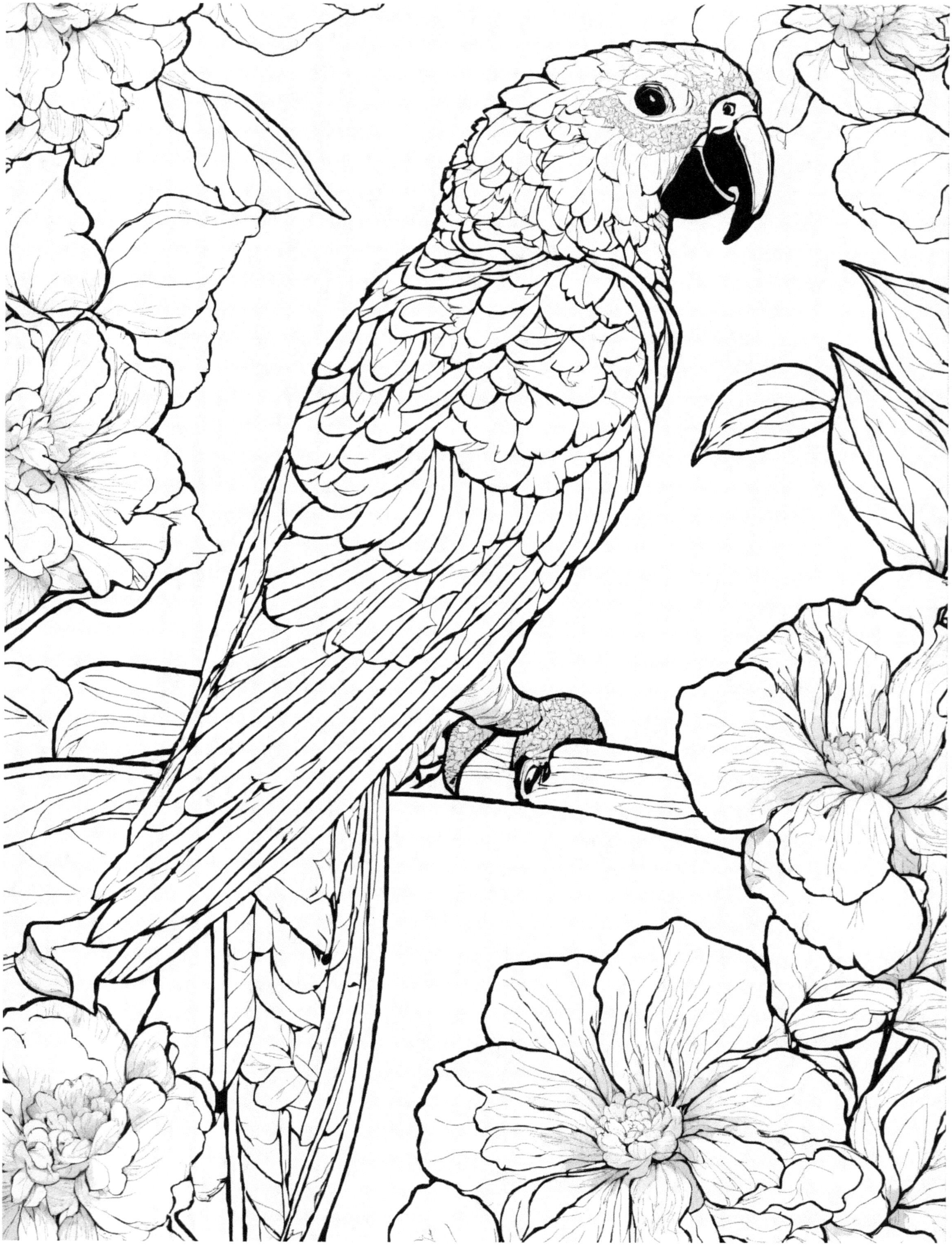

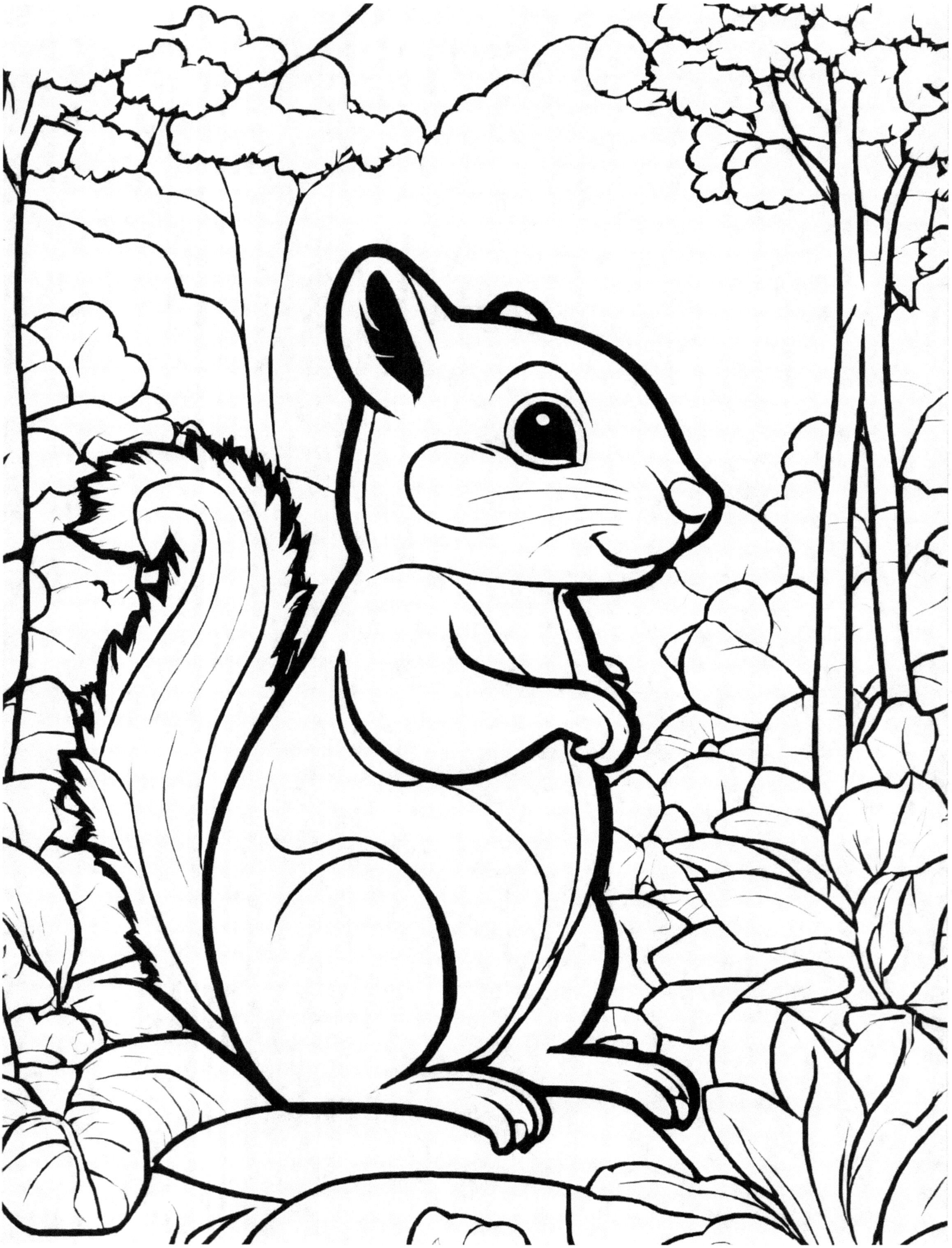

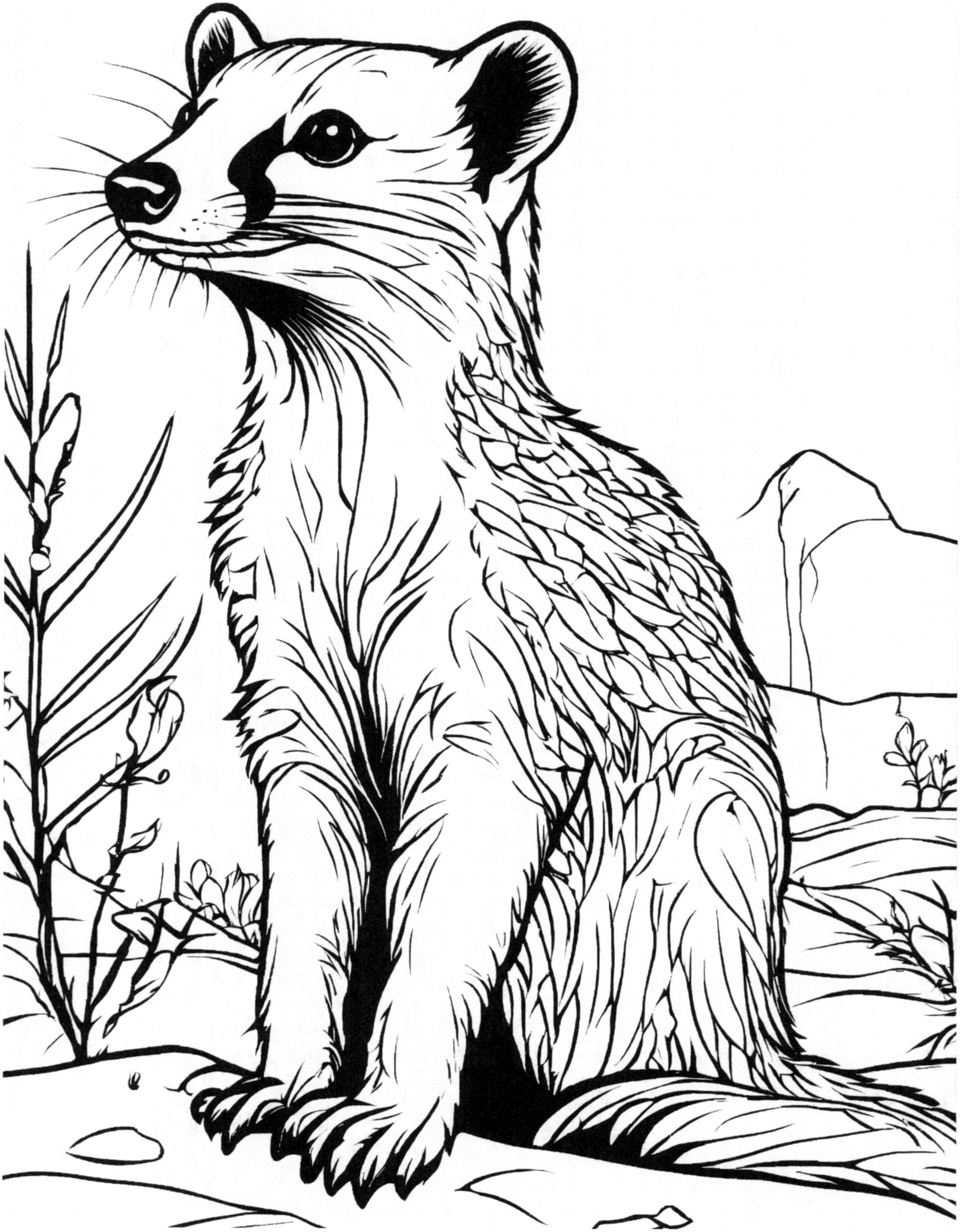

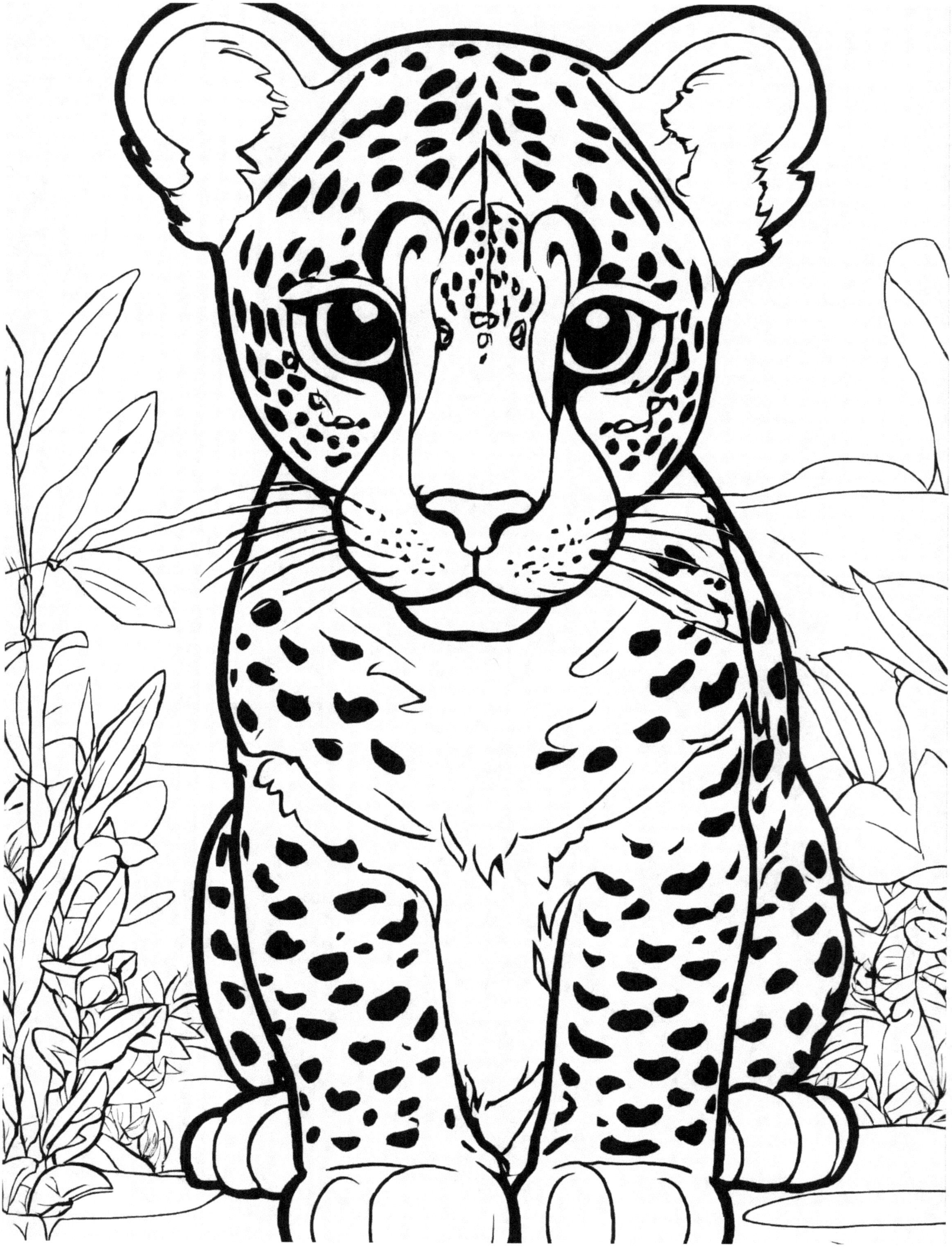

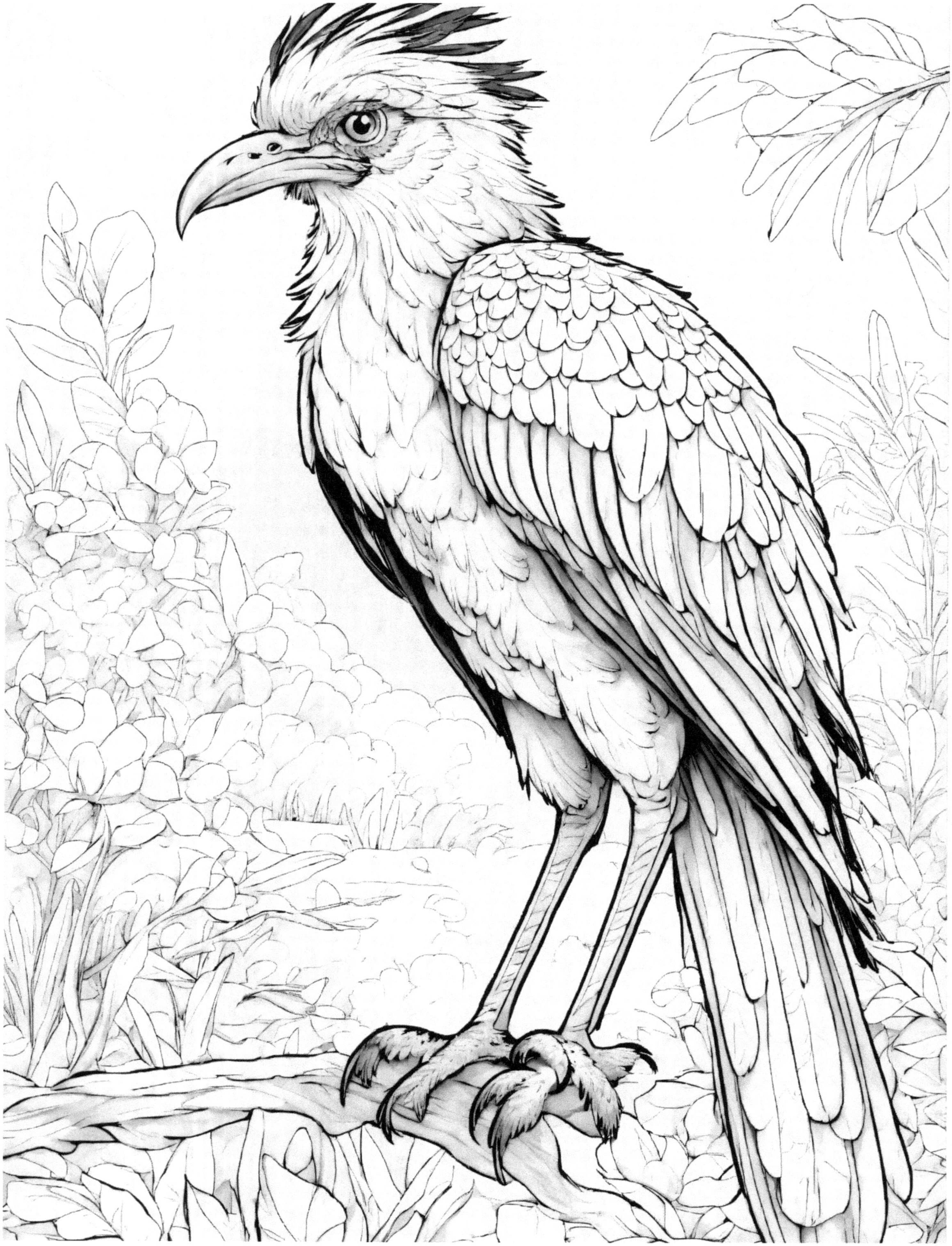

www.ingramcontent.com/pod-product-compliance
Lightning Source LLC
Chambersburg PA
CBHW062120220526
45471CB00010B/3811
* 9 7 9 8 3 2 3 5 9 6 2 6 3 *